John and Lillian Isaacs:

MAKING THE WORD KNOWN

Nell Tyner Bowen

Nell Tyner Bowen
Ps. 34: 7-8
Lillian Isaacs
Matt 6:33

Published by Eagles Publishing Co.
384 Bullsboro Drive #339
Newnan, GA 30263
www.eaglespubs.com

Dedicated

to

The glory of God

With gratitude

to

My husband, I. W.; John; and Lillian

FOREWORD

This story had to be written.

It was born in the heart of God and told through the lives of two people. These two were a "root out of dry ground" (Isaiah 53:2 KJV). They were born in unlikely places for unique stories to begin. Yet, their humble beginnings contributed to the servant lives of their characters.

I have known John and Lillian Isaacs well. They are almost essential to my personal well-being as a Christian. Their personalities are so real, so true to the excellence of Christian living, and so powerful in prayer. They have been very much a part of my own Christian pilgrimage.

Because of their great humility they were reluctant that their story be told. When my good friends from the national WMU headquarters in Birmingham told me that Nell Bowen had been asked to write it, I was overjoyed. Nell is also a longtime personal friend. She is an excellent writer and is sensitive to those things that best exemplify a mission story.

But Lillian and John were hesitant to permit their story to be written. We had to persuade them that it was God's story through the lives of His servants. Only after much prayer would they agree. Nell, Lillian, and John then became joined in the excitement of the journey as the story was written. Literacy missions has come to be seen as evangelism in its finest form. Lillian and John Isaacs are its splendid illustration.

Their home is a refuge. Often after traveling late at night over hazardous roads in the Kentucky mountains, I would "take a night" with them. Their door was always open and there was food to eat. Always there was prayer and concern for some *one* whom God had sent their way. Once as we were visiting a mission Sunday School they were leading, we passed a crippled drunk man sitting beside the road. John said, "I almost despair of winning him to the Lord." A few months later I returned to visit and found the man, born again, and leading the Sunday School class.

You are about to read a contemporary Acts of the Apostles. The leading characters are two evangelists full of wisdom and faith.

M. Wendell Belew

PREFACE

The Home Mission Board called the Isaacs' move from Alaska to Florida in 1972 John's retirement but both he and Lillian knew they simply had followed God's leading to another location. John continued to be God's called person at work in the kingdom.

On december 31, 1983, the Home Mission Board announced Lillian's retirement. Again, the Isaacs knew that retirement does not mean changing who you are. Lillian, also called of God, still works to make the Word known.

Some things do not change!

John and Lillian Isaacs have served together since 1947. Prior to that time they had served individually. Lillian taught school in Alabama, Georgia, and Virginia, while John served as a pastor in Kentucky.

The dates of their service have not been the important factor in their lives, for the message of God's love they have given is timeless. They have worked with persons of all ages, cultures, races, and conditions. They have borne that message to them in season and out of season tirelessly making it a priority of their lives.

Nor have the places of their service been the important factor, for wherever they are, God is there. They listen, and He tells them what He wants them to do. They do it. Wherever they are, exciting stories come forth about persons whose lives are changed by God's power through His Word.

Their experiences, told in the style of one of Lillian's stories, have been hung like well-worn clothes around years and dates, places and events. People are always at the center of each story. This organization is for our clearer understanding of how two unique and strong individuals have been chosen and joined by God and how they complement each other to form an exciting team.

Because of so much demand, and because of current interest in the ministry of literacy, this book is being reprinted. (the Home Mission Board used here is now the North American Mission Board)

Since April 1987 when John Isaacs went to be with the Lord, Lillian has continued this ministry from her home in Tallahassee, Florida.

Updates and many of her recent stories will be given in a forthcoming book, *Lillian Isaacs: Still Making the Word Known.*

CONTENTS

Photo credits
Photos on pages 35, 64, 84, 112, 113, 125, 126, 149, 165, 180, 181, and 204 by North American Mission Board (Formerly Home Mission Board)

Mountain Trails
(1939-1960)

1
The Reverend

The Reverend is back!"
Excited voices carried the news through the little coal-mining town of Haymond.

Everyone knew "The Reverend." He was John Rufus Isaacs, pastor of the Baptist churches at Neon and Haymond. He had come to Kentucky eight years earlier in 1939 at the invitation of Rev. J. S. Bell. The decision to go there had not been easy. Having just graduated from Southern Baptist Theological Seminary, he considered his choices as he sat on the porch of his sister's home in Winston-Salem, North Carolina. He discussed the options with her. Her home had been his home, and he valued her opinion. Should he take the large church offered him, or one of the others that sought him as pastor? Or, should he go to the small congregations in Neon and Haymond, Kentucky?

Nobie Hauser loved her younger brother and wanted him to live near her. She had cared for John because of their mother's poor health when he was an infant. She wanted to continue her ministry to him. She could cook special dishes for him, take care of his clothes, discuss the Scriptures and pray with him, and laugh or cry with him as they remembered their childhood.

But the ultimate decision was John's and the Lord's. And John chose the place where he felt he could serve God best—the hills of Kentucky.

What surprises those two little towns held for the new preacher! And what surprises the new preacher had for his congregations! As a Southern Baptist he believed staunchly in the doctrines taught by his father and his church. In this new setting, not everybody agreed with him. Nevertheless, he remained true to his beliefs, preaching and teaching them regularly.

Neon and Haymond were only three miles apart, but they were in different time zones. So, the Sunday morning services were held at both places at 11:00. The preacher could finish the service at the first church and arrive at the second just in time to deliver his second sermon.

The journey between the two places was not always easy, especially at first. Sometimes Rev. Isaacs rode the bus that carried the miners between towns. Sometimes he walked. Walking the miles between churches was not so bad except in the coldest weather or through winter rains or deep snow. A gift of a heavy overcoat and boots was his only help on many Sundays.

Transportation improved greatly in 1940 when the preacher bought a Model A Ford. He promptly named his $150 purchase "Isaiah," and became known for taking the mountain roads on two wheels as he rushed about conducting the Lord's business.

A part of that business was to pick up about 40 children for Sunday School and take them home after church. Most of them wanted to ride in the rumble seat. That car, loaded with boys and girls, became a familiar sight on the unpaved streets of the little towns.

Isaiah served well for many years, and John sold him for a good price. The day after the sale, however, the car stopped running for good. John explained, "I guess Isaiah just wasn't used to being parked in front of a liquor store, so he self-destructed."

John lived in the church at Haymond, one of the churches he served as pastor. At first the church met in an entertainment hall and boardinghouse provided by the mines for workers who lived out of town. There was a thin partition between the noisy entertainment room and the meeting room of the church. Sunday services did not deter the loud music enjoyed by the miners.

The mining company decided to discontinue the boardinghouse and sell the building. The church members were not upset, for the present arrangement was not good. They saw possibilities in the building and wanted to buy it. With John's leadership, the tiny congregation earned and saved enough money to make payments on their new property. Every dime and dollar was evidence of struggle and sacrifice.

John continued to live in the building, and he made repairs and improvements as money was available. He put together some scraps of wood for a pulpit stand. At the time he said he hoped it would hold together for a few months. As late as 1983, the current pastor still used that pulpit stand at every service.

John loved his people. He wanted to be with them in every situation. At first, when there was a death, he sat with the family at the wake. Later he realized that he was staying up all night sometimes more than once each week. He had to set limits for himself in order to get his work done. He traveled up and down the hollows ministering to his flocks and witnessing to the lost. He was not only the preacher, but also the beloved pastor.

At lunchtime John could usually be found at the

Fleming Cafe enjoying the plate lunch special, followed by a huge slice of apple pie. His favorite places to eat, however, were in the homes of his church members. Frequently he found himself pulling into the yard of Hayes and Althea Crase at just about mealtime.

"Stick a fork into a potato with us," Hayes would say, and the Reverend would pull up a chair and do just that. Althea was a fine Christian mother as well as a good cook. Hayes regularly attended the Neon church, but he had put off making a profession of faith. After a while one of their two daughters went forward in a Sunday morning service requesting baptism and church membership. She was to be baptized that afternoon. John visited with her father again.

"Hayes, you know you ought to make this decision. I believe you will. You might as well just bring your clothes this afternoon and be baptized with Louise."

Hayes made no reply, but to the surprise of the congregation and even his family, he came to the meeting prepared to be baptized.

John and Hayes shared in Bible study, prayer, and Christian fellowship. Hayes gave a testimony to each customer in his barber shop. As he brushed away the stray hairs after a haircut, he commented, "There now. You look good enough to go to church. See you there Sunday."

Another of John's favorite stops was the home of Uncle John and Aunt Tish Arrington. He enjoyed Aunt Tish's delicious cooking, and he liked to hear Uncle John tell of his days in the coal mines store or about how he had courted and won his beautiful bride. The Arringtons were mainstays of the Neon church, and the evening's conversation often turned to questions of doctrine.

"You're a good pastor, Rev. Isaacs," Uncle John would say. "You love us and you care about our children as if they were your own. You're patient with us, and you never give up. You care about our souls."

One day John commented on the service that this deacon gave to the church including cleaning, fuel gathering, bill paying, or whatever was at hand. Uncle John laughed as he explained, "I'm not really a deacon. I just act like one." Years later, after John had left Kentucky, Uncle John Arrington was ordained to the office he had faithfully filled for so long.

When John was in Haymond, he liked to visit in the home of Mrs. Nola Addington and her nine children. Every Sunday Mrs. Addington rounded up the boys and girls early enough to see that they had memorized the verses the preacher had assigned. Often they invited John home for Sunday dinner.

John saw the need for good reading material for his flock, and he started a library at the church. Ruth Addington, one of the younger children, read every book there and asked for more. John provided them whenever he could. Ruth became one of the best read women John ever knew.

In 1941 John added a new dimension to his work. Many teachers had been drafted into the growing army. Others were leaving the area to move to larger cities. John was recruited to teach in the Neon-Fleming School.

"He's a hard teacher," the Addington children reported when the new professor had settled into the classroom.

"We have to behave in his classes," other young people claimed.

"If I ever learn this math," many students added, "I'll never forget it."

Some said, "If I can pass his biology test, I'll know everything!"

The students learned more than math and biology from their new teacher. Gasoline was rationed because of the war. As a minister John was allowed to purchase more gas than most of his students. Some of them tried to persuade him to swap cards or lend them a stamp or two until their next coupon came due. "No one will know," they insisted.

"I will know, and God will know. I will not abuse my privilege as a minister," responded John.

As they drifted away muttering, John thought, "Well, I guess that didn't make me any more popular." But he had earned their respect, and they knew that he wanted what was best for them.

The preacher-teacher stayed busy with his churches and his classroom. The people recognized him as a man of God, but they felt free to give him advice. "Stay out of the alleys, Preacher. Folks who walk there get hurt sometimes." And they felt free to call upon him anytime they needed help. "Reverend, my wife is sick. I wish you'd go see her." Or, "Reverend Isaacs, will you preach the funeral for our grandmother? She don't belong to nobody's church."

John accepted much of their advice, but he walked wherever people were—in alleyways, in the hollows, in the schools, in churches, or at gravesides. Wherever he went, he made friends. Each place served as a pulpit for the message that God loved all people, whatever their condition. The graveside especially became a place of telling the good news of Jesus, and families touched there often responded in John's churches.

Ruth and Norma Addington were children when John Isaacs first came to Haymond. Young, good-looking, energetic, and single, he had attracted every young woman around. The little girls remembered how the single ladies had primped before church services. Ruth and Norma had grown into teenagers in his congregation. They had enjoyed his visits in their home. They had studied the Bible and read missions book under his direction, and their minds were stretched. They had listened to his preaching, and their lives were changed. They had missed him when he left town for a month's vacation. (It was his first vacation from Letcher County in eight years.)

Now he was returning. He had already visited at Neon, for he planned to move into the rooms above the sanctuary there. Excitement ran high as Ruth, Norma, and the others, passed along the news, "The Reverend is back! And he's brought a bride!"

John Isaacs as a seminary student (1936).

2
Rebecca

A T LAST, summer had come (1945). The mountain children looked forward to the extra church activities. There would be additional Bible studies, special outings, and of course, Vacation Bible School. A volunteer summer worker was coming to help with these additional activities at Fleming, Neon, and Haymond Baptist Churches.

Brother Galloway, the pastor at Fleming, was set to meet the bus bringing the worker, but he got busy and could not go. The task, therefore, fell to Rev. Isaacs. He had instructions to take the young woman to lunch before settling her at her lodging for the summer.

John waited for the bus door to open and viewed each passenger who stepped off. One of them especially caught his eye. She was tall and slender and wore a perky black hat. He asked the driver if a Miss Kirtland had arrived on his bus. To his delight, the lovely woman with the hat overheard his question and identified herself as the Vacation Bible School worker.

The cafe's splendid lunch was not as interesting to John as it usually was. The young woman held him spellbound. He was thinking that missions work is not always dull. Sometimes it has beautiful brown eyes. He learned quickly that Miss Kirtland was a missions volunteer and much interested in Africa.

As the summer went by, John was increasingly attracted to this intelligent young woman. Her sparkling eyes kept his attention, and he liked her quick mind and her sense of humor. She was a good worker too, and her Bible school classes were very creative. She knew the Word and loved to teach it.

By the end of the summer, John knew that he could love Miss Kirtland. But the ever-present thought of Africa dashed his hopes of marriage. So he just enjoyed her company until time for her to leave.

For Lillian Kirtland, leaving meant returning to Giles County, Virginia, to teach school. She was a natural born teacher. Actually she had started her teaching career almost simultaneously with her formal education.

As a precocious and eager child, she had learned to read at three years of age. Her mother had been a teacher until the children began to come along. She and Lillian's father encouraged all of the children, and they all knew the value of education. Lillian talked little and listened much. Almost without realizing it, she learned from her older brother and sisters everything they learned in school. One sister showed her numbers, another showed her how to print the alphabet, and another taught her to spell. After much persuasion, her brother shared his American history lessons with her. She promised to do, and did, most of Max's farm chores in exchange for this coveted information. Lillian worked in the fields along with her father and the other children in the summer. She listened as her father told stories—all of the classics as well as Bible stories—or as the group chanted multiplication tables and spelled words or swapped facts.

Her father's stories inspired her most of all. The children had to work fast in order to keep up with him. At the end of a row of chopping cotton or hoeing corn, he would finish the story. They all wanted to be there to hear. Lillian learned not only the stories, but also the skills that make storytellers successful. Occasionally she practiced on her family, but more often she practiced on the chickens and guineas.

Lillian's first day in school was a near disaster. For the first few minutes the teacher was busy with housekeeping chores such as getting desks assigned, tying shoes, and calming first grade jitters. The children seemed unable to be quiet, and the teacher seemed unable to make them do so. In the middle of the confusion, Lillian raised her hand and asked, "Just what are we going to do in school?"

"Learn to read and write," came the harried but obvious answer.

"And what if I can already read and write?" Lillian asked next.

The frustrated teacher saw a problem in the making and decided to put an end to these questions. Picking up a newspaper from her desk, she instructed Lillian to come forward and read. For the first time, there was silence.

"Which paragraph?" asked Lillian.

Indignant and still unbelieving, the teacher chose at random. Lillian began to read clearly and accurately. Before she finished the paragraph, the teacher interrupted. "You go on up to the second grade."

To Lillian's chagrin, she discovered that she had already read many of the books used in the combination second and third grades. There were other interesting happenings in that room, however, and she settled down to being happy in school. She pulled her chair up close to the teacher's desk and explained, "Miss Lizzie, I'm in your class, and I want to be close to where you are." Lillian never mentioned her change of grades at home, and everyone supposed that she was in the proper one.

Lillian soon noticed eight or ten boys and girls who sat to one side of the room. Most of them were larger than the other children, and they seldom participated in class activities. The other children ignored them in class and avoided them at recess. "Why don't these children get their books and do what everybody else does?" Lillian wanted to know.

"They don't have any books," Miss Lizzie replied.

"How can they learn then?"

"They can't learn."

"Well, I can already read these books we're reading now. I can teach 'em to read. Please let me try." With that simple request, Lillian launched her teaching career. She copied pages from her own books and passed them to "her class." She wrote words on paper scraps, on the backs of calendar pages, on anything she could find.

She stood by their sides as they read. That way she was the same height as they were sitting down. "Here, you can read that word. Good, good," she would whisper in their ears.

Her biggest problem came in a story that had *Sh-h-h* in it. The children stopped every time they saw it, not knowing what that funny word was. Lillian would prompt them, "Sh-h-h." They became still and quiet and said nothing. They could not understand what their little teacher was trying to tell them. Finally, in desperation, Lillian almost shouted, "*Sh-h-h* is a word. Say it. Everybody say *Sh-h-h.*" Even Miss Lizzie had to laugh.

"Miss Lizzie, my class doesn't have pencils and paper for arithmetic lessons," reported Lillian.

"They're too poor to buy those things," the teacher replied sadly.

Lillian shared her own tablets, broke her pencils

in half, and begged for more supplies at home.

"Miss Lizzie," Lillian observed one day, "they don't have any lunch, and lots of 'em say they don't have any breakfast. They're hungry!"

"I'm sorry, Lillian," the teacher spoke softly and slowly, "I just can't help you with that."

The next morning, after a big breakfast, Lillian explained to her mother how hungry she got at school. Her mother made her a bigger lunch. The lunches grew as she reported being hungrier each day. If nobody was looking, Lillian put the extra breakfast biscuits in her lunch sack. Eventually, each of "her children" had something for lunch. Lillian never ate at school.

All year long the little teacher encouraged her class. She sat with them, played with them at recess, and taught them. Most of all she loved them. At the end of the year she explained to Miss Lizzie that she expected all of her class to be promoted. To the teacher's amazement, all of those non-learners were working on grade level. Each of them was promoted to the third grade.

Lillian was promoted to the fourth grade. She missed her class. During the summer she had again read ahead of her grade, and the new teacher had nothing for her to do. She was bored and ill at ease. One day, about three weeks into the school year, she simply moved back into the third grade, announced her presence to Miss Lizzie, and picked up her teaching duties.

One of the saddest days in her first year had been field day. None of "her class" had been able to do anything well enough to make points. Lillian had written down all of the events of the day. When she came back to her class, she had practice every day at recess. They did three-legged races, carried potatoes in a spoon, relayed sticks to their partners, and hopped in sacks. When field day came again, Lillian's class took top honors for the whole school.

Her charges continued to learn, and most went

with her to the fourth grade the next year.

Lillian continued to develop her talent as a story-teller. She told stories she had heard from her father as well as those she had read for herself.

When she went to Mercer University in Macon, Georgia, she had already read (and written reports for) all of the required books her three years there. She took extra courses, including Greek. As the only woman in a class of preachers-in-training, she excelled. Soon she became a substitute teacher in that class.

In spite of extra courses with recognized authorities and outside work to support herself, Lillian graduated summa cum laude. She was a member of Cardinal Key, the highest honor given to a female student by the university.

Degree in hand, Lillian took her first paying teaching job in Bon Air, Georgia. After two years of paying off college bills and saving what she could, Lillian went to the WMU Training School at Louisville, Kentucky. Georgia WMU gave her a scholarship which made her further education possible.

After graduation from seminary Lillian lived for a year in Alabama, and then moved to Virginia. This would be her third year of teaching Bible in the Giles County schools.

The first year after Lillian left Kentucky moved fairly quickly for John. He always kept busy, even if he had something (or someone) different on his mind. He and Isaiah traveled through red and yellow leaves and watched them drop with the coming of winter, but he could not forget the tall girl and her sparkling eyes, set off by that crazy hat. He began to write to her, and thinking of her as being in a far country, he began each of those letters, "Dear Rebecca."

Lillian stayed busy too. She applied for missions work in Africa and went for a physical examination.

Tests showed that she could not tolerate the rigors of an equatorial country. Her application was turned down.

How strange! Lillian knew that God wanted her in missions. Her call was clear. She had recognized this call when she was 11 years old. Even before she had made a public profession of faith or became a church member, she had been a missions volunteer.

As a child she had attended the churches and Sunday Schools of her community. From her early years she had read her Bible every day. She knew that God loved her, and she loved Him. They talked as parent and child, for she had given her life to Him.

"Father, could I have misunderstood Your directions? Is there something else You want me to do? Or, do You want me to be a missionary somewhere else?"

Lillian shared some of these thoughts with John. The news that Lillian wasn't going to Africa gave John new hope. "Dear Rebecca" letters moved with a lilt from his pen. By the time the dogwood blossomed in the spring, Isaiah and the Reverend had found business in Danville several times. The visits were short, squeezed between church and teaching duties. But on one of those visits, John carried a ring that sparkled to match Lillian's eyes.

As he slipped the ring onto Lillian's finger, she found the answer to the question that she had carried in her heart since she first met John at the Fleming bus station. Her missions field would be at home, and she would serve with the husband God had chosen especially for her.

John and Lillian visited family members in Alabama, Tennessee, and North Carolina. On August 20, 1947, a quiet ceremony in the First Baptist Church of Oak Ridge, Tennessee, gave John Isaacs his Rebecca.

Lillian (left) and her sister Grace at ages five and three.

Newlyweds John and Lillian in Neon, Kentucky (1947).

3
Team at Work

LILLIAN quickly became a part of the communities where John had worked alone. The people remembered her from her summer of VBS work, and they accepted her now as their pastor's wife. The front seat of the car had one more passenger on many of its trips. John's quick lunches shifted to mealtime conferences as the couple shared, planned, and worked together. They shared the joys and burdens of Sunday School and church responsibilities. John now had a helper who complemented his talents and strengths. They made a strong team as each inspired confidence in the other. They had the common purpose of doing God's will.

"John, you study and preach; I'll do the family bookkeeping."

"Lillian, you take care of the meals; I'll take care of the transportation."

And they volunteered for each other. "That day will be fine for the Bible study. Of course John will be happy to teach it."

"We must have a strong missionary emphasis. Certainly Lillian will be glad to teach the book."

One Saturday, after a morning of visiting, John went down to the Fleming Cafe for lunch. He skimmed the menu for the 35-cent special, thought about that steaming hot apple pie for one more nickel, and made up his mind without further hesitation. He could almost taste the ham-flavored beans and crisp fried chicken as he chatted with other waiting diners. Just as his appetite sharpened to the point of a sweet agony, the waitress placed his food before him. He said a quick grace and lifted a forkful of buttery mashed potatoes to his mouth.

"Hello, Reverend," came a familiar drawl. "Where's the bride today?"

Suddenly the potatoes tasted like cotton. Where was his bride? For a brief moment he had forgotten he had one. Washing down the potatoes, he made some excuse about how busy she was at home. The aroma of the hot lunch and the accompanying pie now vied for his attention—and won. John reasoned that Lillian would understand that he should not waste the food he had ordered. He ate quickly, trying not to cause further questions, and excused himself to take care of important business at home.

It was years before Lillian learned why John's appetite was so poor that first time he came in late for lunch.

On another occasion, Lillian decided at the last minute that she just must have some sliced tomatoes to complete her menu. After announcing her mission, she set off to buy some.

"It's a good thing I wouldn't let John tell me what people say about everybody in town," she thought as she smiled at each neighbor she passed. "I'm sure I'll form enough prejudices on my own." Just then she spied a basket of lucious red tomatoes in a store across the street. "It's a good thing, too, I told him I'd shop wherever I want to," she half giggled as she entered the strange little market.

As the door closed behind her, she heard a rough voice whisper loudly, "Who in the world is that?"

29

"It's The Reverend's new wife," another voice replied.

From the back room of the store came sounds of shuffling feet and a slamming door. Lillian noticed that the shelves had little to offer except the merchandise in the window.

The store owner came smiling from the back room. Bowing low, he slicked down his hair with one hand. "Howdy ma'am. And how's The Reverend today?"

"Hello," Lillian smiled back. "He's fine, thank you."

"What can I do for you today?"

"I'd like to buy some tomatoes."

"Oh, some tomatoes?" He moved toward the window. "Do you think these will do?"

"Yes, I think so," Lillian ventured as she felt the firm red skins. "I'll take these four. Now, how much do I owe you?"

"Oh, not a thing! You take 'em—take the whole basket—with my best wishes. And be sure to give my regards to The Reverend." He bowed again as he talked.

"Thank you," Lillian replied with a big smile. "We'd love to have you come to our church next Sunday."

Obviously surprised by the invitation, the storekeeper cleared his throat. "Maybe I just will. And you come back any time you see tomatoes in the window!"

"What a nice fellow," Lillian thought as she almost skipped home.

When John sat down to lunch, Lillian reported on the kind man in the store and the gift of tomatoes. John's fork stopped in midair. "Where did you say you got these tomatoes?"

"From the little store down at the edge of town. And I invited that kind fellow to come to church."

John dropped his fork to his plate and swallowed hard. "That 'kind fellow' you just invited to church is the best known bootlegger in the county. And we're eating his notice that he has a fresh batch of whiskey for sale." Somehow John's appetite lessened a bit.

Lillian ate on calmly. "He *is* a kind fellow! And of all people, he needs to be in church next Sunday. I hope he comes."

If John was surprised at Lillian's openness, she was no less surprised at some of John's approaches to meeting people's needs. When school opened Lillian began teaching. This shortened the amount of time she and John had for planning together. On Wednesday evening before their first Thanksgiving together, as they drove to prayer meeting, John announced that he had invited company for dinner the next day.

"Oh?" replied Lillian. "How many?" She had made no preparation for a holiday meal.

John replied casually. "I asked all the teachers from Georgia and other far off places who couldn't get home for the holidays—three of them, I think. And their boyfriends. I guess that's about six. And there may be some others."

"What do you want us to serve?"

"Turkey and all the trimmings. And sweet potatoes," was John's calm answer.

Lillian felt her stomach tighten. She had never claimed to be a good cook, or even an ordinary cook, for that matter. During the service she planned a menu and tried to think of a grocery store that would be open late that night.

They found a store, bought the groceries, and went home. The day had been long, so Lillian simply stored the food and went to bed. By morning she realized she needed to started cooking immediately. She also realized the frozen turkey should have been thawing all night. A total of ten guests were coming. She wondered how they would get everybody in the tiny apartment above Neon church and if the floor would collapse with so many

31

people walking around. Suddenly she realized she must get chairs and dishes from somewhere to take care of the crowd.

The morning passed too rapidly. Guests who came at noon milled around and drank lemonade or coffee for hours. At four o'clock, Lillian decided in desperation to serve dinner as it was. The turkey was well done on one side and nearly raw on the other. The green peas were as hard as the chinaberries the children threw at each other in the summer. The rice stuck together and had to be sliced before it was served. The cake split in the middle while icing ran off the sides. But the sweet potatoes were perfect, and so was the fellowship! From that day John and Lillian knew that holidays would always be special in their home. The sharing of love and fellowship is more important than fancy food eaten at a banquet table.

As John and Lillian ministered to the people, time raced by. In the summer, they had almost continuous Vacation Bible Schools, sometimes at three different places in one day. One summer they held at least 20 schools.

The children loved their pastor and his wife. The girls giggled as they swapped hair ribbons or in other ways tried to confuse Lillian as to their identity. Both boys and girls liked the missions reading programs, the Bible memory work, activities in GA and RA, and the trips that John planned for them. Jonelle Collier came to visit almost every day just after school. She found a second home at the Isaacs' house. There the pastor and his wife taught the young people who gathered. They shared solutions for problems and gave directions for lives. Like Jonelle, many of them dedicated their lives and their talents to serving God—following the Issacs' example. Like their parents, they believed they had the best preacher and pastor of any church in Kentucky—maybe the whole United States.

John stayed busy in the community. He was the one called when there was a death. Many times he made friends at such occasions. He talked with the people in charge, and with relatives and friends of the deceased. One such person was "The Little Chief," police chief for the town of Neon. He was responsible for traffic at funerals, and faded in and out of the church as the service was being held. He was polite to the Isaacs, but he kept his distance.

In her fourth year of teaching, Lillian was given a special class. Many of the pupils seemed to have learning problems. She was reminded of her first class, and quickly named her charges "the opportunity class." She made them feel so special and so important and so loved that each child blossomed with talents.

The class members made a set of rules to guide their conduct, and there were no discipline problems. Rewards for good work abounded. At church and at school these children thrived on drama. Joe and Sue, who learned to spell, were allowed to be script writers. Ann, Mike, and Tom, who finally learned their math facts, became bankers or brokers or merchants. Rex and Howard, Sarah and Betty, good readers, became prompters and directors. Good singers who had excelled in the Bible memory verses played the parts of angels in the Christmas play. One child who learned to paint made backdrops and lettered cue cards.

Lillian remembered her own sadness when, as a child, she did not have a part in the school play. She was allowed, however, to watch rehearsals. As she watched, she memorized every part and made a copy of the script. On the day of the play the teacher lost her copy. The cast was distressed. Who would prompt them if they forgot a line? Lillian came to the rescue. She volunteered to be the prompter. Although she did not not need it, she produced her handwritten script to give them added security.

Lillian never forgot that feeling of being left out. Every child in her class had a part in every play. Mamas and papas flocked to school. Children sharpened their skills and memories with facts and stories they had disdained in textbooks. Grades pulled upward. It seemed that 1951 would be the best year yet.

Lillian went to school each day as usual in spite of hoarseness and a sore throat. Afternoons were full of church activities. Then one day as the class sat with pencils poised for a spelling contest, their whole world changed. Mrs. Isaacs opened her mouth to speak, but no sounds came! She tried again. Still no sound!

One by one the pupils raised their heads and saw with horror that their beloved teacher could make no sound at all. A funereal silence settled over the room. They managed to take directions from Lillian's strained whisper and notes scrawled on the blackboard. When school was over they left, still wrapped in the unnatural quiet that accompanies disaster.

John was worried and immediately sought the doctor. After the usual examinations, the verdict came.

"You are exhausted! Your vocal cords are covered with ulcers. You must take this medication, and you must rest in bed," he said firmly as he scratched illegible directions on a prescription pad, "and above all, you must not talk!" Lillian felt as though a new law had been written and it could not be changed. The medication, the bed rest, and the silence were absolutes.

Haymond Baptist Church where John was pastor.

A truck loaded with coal driving along a mountain road in Eastern Kentucky.

4
New Directions

ALL previous ministry patterns changed. John's voice was the only one heard at home or at church. Along the way, he had become interim pastor for two other churches, McRoberts Baptist Church and Fleming Baptist Church. When Lillian became ill, John was responsible for four churches, each having a full-time program. He arranged his Sundays and weekdays so he could be at the right church at the right time.

Some changes were taking place in the four churches when Lillian became ill. Members at the Neon church felt they were too small and too weak financially to continue a complete church program. So they sold their new building and joined nearby congregations. McRoberts was at the point of securing a full-time pastor to meet their growing needs.

Fleming Baptist Church still shared John with the church at Haymond. Fleming had Sunday evening worship and Training Union on Sunday nights. Haymond had Training Union on Tuesday and preaching on Thursday evenings. Both churches had prayer meeting on Wednesday evenings.

Woman's Missionary Union and Brotherhood remained strong at both Fleming and Haymond.

There was one big difference. The work that Lillian had been doing for these churches was assumed by volunteers or by John.

In order to keep Lillian in bed, John became housekeeper, cook, grocery shopper, and bearer of news to and from home. These duties he manned cheerfully, often singing or quoting Bible verses as he performed them.

Lillian's students missed her. They felt nobody understood them the way she did. They liked the plays she wrote for them and the Bible verses she taught them. In fact, school was fun and exciting when she was there. Substitute teachers tried to use books and harsh words to get their attention. Discipline became a problem again. Once the boys "lost" the door to their room and "could not study because of the noise and the cold." Lillian insisted they find the door and put it on its hinges again. They visited her and begged her to return.

"We'll carry you on your bed. You won't have to move at all. You won't have to talk. We'll be quiet as mice. Please come back to us!"

Lillian wanted to return to her class but could not. She was unable to talk above a whisper and felt weak most of the time. Somehow the school year ended.

"Lord, thank You for making me rest," she prayed as she lay still and quiet for the first few days. "I am so tired, but I know I'll be rested soon. And thank You for making my throat well! I know You will. I'll be back at Your work soon."

The resting days grew in number, however, for the vocal cords did not heal as rapidly as she had hoped. Days stretched into weeks, and then into months.

Instead of bemoaning her enforced bed rest, Lillian was thrilled with the quiet time she had. She had talked with God since she was a tiny child.

37

Now there was just more time to do it.

As John came and went she wrote notes for him.

"Please mail these cards for me. I've made one—with Scripture verses—for every patient at the leprosy hospital."

"Oh, John, I loved my new cookie surprise!"

"Leave a list of the patients at the hospital. I'll have plenty of time today to pray for each one."

"Save time to tell me about the meeting at the church this morning. You forgot to tell me about the Jones' new baby."

"Mail these thank you notes when you get the mail."

"Please check out these books for me at the library."

Library books again became a great pleasure. Lillian had not read so many since she was in high school. She read avidly then and was eager to learn. She even borrowed her sister's list of required college textbooks. By the time Lillian went to college she had read all of the required books, and had made written reports on them.

She smiled as she remembered filling her suitcase with those reports. She almost laughed as she thought, "That was certainly all right. I didn't have enough clothes to fill it. And wasn't God good to me? He gave me so many jobs, I barely had time to read the textbooks. He certainly took care of me! If He took such good care of me then, I know He's taking care of my throat and vocal cords now. I just won't worry about that."

The most enjoyable parts of the day, however, were those hours spent reading the Bible. Lillian worked out a plan for reading from both the Old Testament and New Testament each day. Whole chapters came alive as she read. It seemed she could hear God speaking to her each time she opened her Bible. The sweetness of this fellowship grew. She knew God heard and understood her voiceless prayers.

One day she was thanking God for the ability to read. "Father, being able to read is the most wonderful blessing! Next to my own salvation, reading is my greatest gift from you."

While praying, Lillian remembered the time a neighboring farmer came to get her father to fill out some papers. After seeing this friend's X on a check, Mr. Kirtland called his daughter to show this grown man how to write his name. Mr. Kirtland spelled the name for Lillian, and she wrote it on her tablet. She went outside to the big oak tree where the neighbor was resting and printed on the ground. As he traced the letters with his finger, the neighbor learned to read and write his own name. He took the paper from her tablet with him. "I will look at my name again and again and remember how to write it!" he said as he patted the folded treasure in his pocket.

Lillian also remembered Aunt Susie. "Lillian, it's time to take the newspapers and this hot food to Aunt Susie. And be sure to read her mail for her." Lillian could almost hear her mother calling her. She remembered how the cool bark of the foot log felt as she crossed the creek to Aunt Susie's house. Aunt Susie's eyes would light up when someone read to her. And Lillian remembered the walls lined with newspapers. Where there were no pictures, the pages were upside down. She remembered that even as a child she knew Aunt Susie could not read.

The prodding of the Holy Spirit caused Lillian to remember others who could not read, and she felt a wave of deep sadness sweep over her. "What can I do about it, God?"

When that afternoon was over, Lillian knew that God had a plan for opening His written Word to many nonreading adults. And she knew, too, that she was to be a part of that plan.

Lillian's body grew stronger before her voice came back. She could be up some of the time, but had to remain silent. One afternoon she felt God leading her to take copies of the book of John to one of the hospitals to give them to every person who passed her.

Not being able to converse, she just smiled as she handed out Scripture portions. One of the persons who came by was The Little Chief. He accepted the book and returned the smile. It was a well-known fact that he was not a Christian, nor a real churchgoer. "Reverend," he would say as John witnessed to him, "you just go on and believe whatever you want. Religion is not for me. I'm a good man, and I got all the help I need right here." He patted his holster and laughed.

The Little Chief had begun to like John and Lillian. He joked about Lillian's silence. "At least you can't invite me to church." He came by their house to get help with problems in a math course he was taking by correspondence. He drank coffee and said he felt at home with John and Lillian. The Isaacs loved him and longed to have him know their Saviour, but he kept resisting.

The seasons changed. Another school year started and Christmas passed. Lillian remained silent, and rested—much of the time in bed. When the last chill of spring had left, however, she began to feel her strength return. Her voice came back and she was no longer bedridden. She could begin working again, but never would she be the same. In those two years of silence, God had given her a new direction for her life.

Meanwhile, John too had become aware of stirrings in his own life. New opportunities opened to him. In 1952 he became director of missions in the Pine Mountain Association (of Kentucky). His knowledge of the hills and their peoples had prepared him uniquely to be the pastor of the pastors who served with him. They came to him for advice and counseling, for fellowship and renewal, for training and new ideas. But most of all, they came

40

to him for instruction and teaching from God's Word.

Life was full and exciting as God revealed new avenues of service for John and Lillian. Then in September 1953 He gave them a special blessing—a child. John held his little son and thought back to his own childhood. As the baby of the family, his parents and older brother and sister had made him feel speical. John's father had taught him at home. He recalled how he and his siblings learned a portion of the Scriptures each day. His father demanded perfection in every subject, but especially in the Scriptures. "There was no wiggling or noise in that room," he whispered to tiny John Rufus Isaacs XV who had started to squirm and cry.

Now it was Lillian's turn to reminisce as she comforted and fed her baby. She was next to the youngest girl in a family of five sisters and one brother. She was so tiny and sickly at first that all were afraid she would not live. "God made you beautiful—so healthy and perfect," she whispered to Johnny as she felt his pink fingers curl around her own. "I hope those fingers can draw like your grandfather, John Rufus Isaacs XIII. Maybe you'll draw beautiful birds like he did. And I pray you will use all the talents God has given you for His glory."

The household changed immediately to accommodate Johnny's presence and needs. Major changes were in the making, however, before his second birthday.

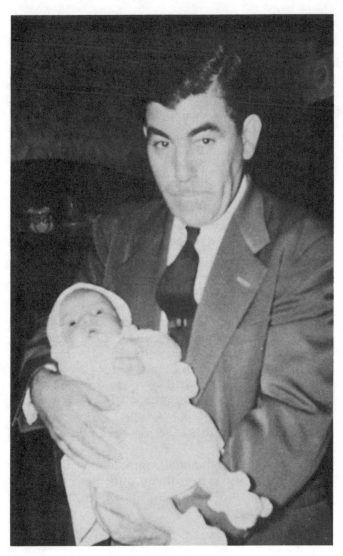

John and Johnny (1953).

5
Adventures at Clear Creek

John Isaacs' reputation as a Bible teacher grew. In 1955 he was invited to become a professor at Clear Creek Baptist School in Pineville, Kentucky. The position seemed perfect for him. He was a natural teacher, grounded from birth in the Scriptures. In addition, he understood many of the problems that brought students to Clear Creek. He understood other problems they faced when they arrived. Many had not finished high school. Still fewer had attended college. They came leaving jobs, but still having families to support. When they felt God's call to the ministry, they came to Clear Creek to prepare to answer that call.

John had experienced a similar struggle. He dropped out of Wilkerson (North Carolina) High School in the middle of the ninth grade. The glamour of being a cowboy pulled him to his twin uncles' farm in Texas. The glamour began to change to drudgery, however, as he plowed, planted, and picked cotton.

John became a Christian at age 14. After spending many hours conversing with God, John heard the call to preach. His first sermons were preached to

43

his cotton crop. He finished high school at Howard Payne Academy and went on to Howard Payne College. He worked to pay his way through both high school and college.

Again, without funds, he went on faith to Louisville, Kentucky, in 1935 to enter Southern Baptist Theological Seminary. Previous work experience in a hospital in Texas landed John a job as attendant in the seminary infirmary.

Weekends saw John Isaacs with a congregation near Cincinnati, Ohio. "I could have used a little more money, a little more food and clothes. Some may have thought I was having a hard time. But if I was, I didn't know about it. I knew there were a lot of conversions. And I knew that preaching, going to school, and working were all going to be helpful later in my ministry."

Lillian, too, understood how hard school can be for students who must work to support themselves. She had worked at as many as three jobs at one time to make ends meet. She decided to help students at Clear Creek or their spouses find employment, even if it had to be in her own home.

The family settled into a native stone house near the Clear Creek campus. John taught during the week and preached on the weekends at the Baptist church across Fonde Mountain in the little mining village of Fonde.

Lillian became involved in campus life, especially with activities that included students wives. They seemed to be drawn to her as she was to them.

The cold winter brought its usual sniffles and colds to the Isaacs family. Even by spring Lillian seemed unable to shake her symptoms. She also seemed unable to make the house feel dry from the season's rains and snows. She fought the dampness, and she fought to feel good. She was successful in neither battle.

In a few weeks Lillian became sick enough to stay in bed. Her doctor thought in time she would be better, but time proved she needed something more. She was dangerously ill from the infection that attacked her body. Finally, she was moved to a hospital where doctors agreed that surgery must be performed immediately in order to save her life.

It was a desperate time. Lillian saw John's worried face and heard loved ones cry. She seemed to come and go between two worlds. Ordinarily she would have worried about John and Johnny being left alone to look after themselves, but a peace surrounded her. As she talked with God He assured her of His care for her family. He assured her of her calling to teach people to read. It seemed that her unfinished task for Him on earth was pitted against the blessedness of heaven.

While the doctors thought she was unconscious, they discussed her condition. "I don't think she'll ever make it through surgery," one said to the other.

"Nor do I," came the hushed reply.

Lillian smiled to herself. She had a guarantee from a greater physician—the only one who can heal.

Convalescence was slow and long. At times it was sad. Lillian lost the child she was carrying and hope of any others.

Lillian regained her strength slowly. Even before she had become so sick, consistent attendance at the Fonde Church had been almost impossible. Neither she nor Johnny fared well on the 30 miles of mountain curves, and the long day without rest was too much. They attended Sunday School and worship services at the First Baptist Church in nearby Pineville. For special services they went to Fonde with John.

One such special occasion happened unexpectedly. While Lillian rested one Sunday afternoon, Johnny played quietly with his toys. Both were startled when a loud knock came at the door. Lillian straightened her hair as she came through the living room. "Johnny, pick up your toys from the middle

45

of the floor. We've got company."

Lillian opened the door and greeted the Phipps family. The Isaacs had known The Little Chief and his wife and two small sons in Fleming.

The Phipps family and Lillian visited for a while. They told Lillian about their move from Fleming to Tennessee. The Little Chief seemed restless. Finally he asked, "Where's The Reverend? Will he be here soon?"

"He's preaching over at Fonde, you know," Lillian said. And he doesn't come home on Sunday afternoons."

"Oh," he replied, his smile suddenly gone. "I knew he preached over there. In fact, we tried to find the church last Sunday, but took a wrong turn and ended up in Tennessee. Thought maybe he'd be here in the afternoon."

"Would you like to go over there for the evening service?" Lillian ventured. "Johnny and I can go and show you the way."

Lillian thought to herself, "He'd never go to church back at Neon-Fleming."

The Little Chief brightened. "Yes, that would be great. That's why I've come."

Lillian quickly made sandwiches for them, and got Johnny ready for church. Then all six got into the car for the long trip over the mountain. The children's comments furnished the only conversation as they rode. The Little Chief seemed to have something on his mind. His wife closed her eyes and pretended not to see how the road curved and seemed to drop off the side of the mountain. Lillian was deep in her own thoughts. "What's bothering The Little Chief?" she wondered. "He seems different, or quiet, or something. I'll just pray for him."

Finally they arrived, parked, and walked toward the beautiful white building. The Little Chief led the way as they marched down the aisle. "This seems a little strange," Lillian thought to herself.

"We're sitting on the second row!"

John was surprised but happy to see all of them. His sermon came from Isaiah 53. Many in the congregation were moved to tears. When they stood to sing the hymn of decision, The Little Chief stepped forward and made a public profession of his faith.

The service was a time of great rejoicing. Afterwards, The Little Chief and his family went back to Pineville to spend the night with the Isaacs. He told them what led him to make his decision.

"I've always liked being at your house," The Little Chief began. "But I felt funny at first—being in a preacher's house. I didn't know if it was really me or not," he chuckled. Then more seriously, he went on, "You remember, pretty soon after you gave me that book of John, Lillian, I came to tell you about reading it. In fact, I memorized just about all of it while I was a guard at the coal tipple [a coal-screening plant]. It'd get quiet as the night wore on, and I'd get that little book out and read it every night. Meant a lot to me!"

"Yes, and we wanted so much for you to give your heart to the Lord then," John added quietly, "but you said, 'Not now.' "

"Reverend," confessed The Little Chief, "you could never know how I watched you every day—at the parking meter, at the gas station, around town. I tried to see if you were any better than me, or as honest as I was. I checked to see if you paid your bills. I wanted to know if my life would be better if I gave it to Jesus. I couldn't find you doing wrong anytime! And I heard a lot more at all those funerals than you thought I did. That book of John—the Word of God and the testimony of your life! That's what won me!"

Mrs. Phipps, The Little Chief's wife, had been listening as they talked. She had never made a profession of faith. "That's sort of what I've been doing at home," she stated quietly. "When you told me you were a Christian now, I sort of smiled to myself and said, 'I'll just wait and see if you're any different." Well you are! I want to be a Christian too."

Indeed she had been listening through the sermon and all the talking. After reading the Scriptures and praying, she, too, accepted Jesus as Saviour and Lord.

"Reverend," The Little Chief said almost as though he were thinking out loud. "I want you to baptize me. Do you think you could arrange it at Fleming so I could give a witness there about what Jesus means to me? I want to invite my friends to see me follow Him in baptism."

By now the earliest streaks of a rising sun were lighting the sky. The day had been long, but the joy of all that had happened seemed to make these friends want to talk even longer.

The baptismal service was arranged in the Fleming church. The building was packed with those who wanted to see and hear the testimony of their beloved Little Chief.

Long before the end of his first teaching year, John Isaacs had become known on the campus as a stiff professor. The students also called him gentle and encouraging, but there were absolutes they learned to respect.

"Your assignment is to learn from memory these three verses that were the basis for the lesson we studied today," he would tell his class in Baptist doctrine. Then as though echoing his father's instructions, "You must make no mistakes, for each one will lower your grade by five points."

The students protested at first and insisted they could not learn verses from memory. But they did. Mr. Isaacs stuck by his rule that the verses must be written perfectly—each *the*, *and*, and *evenso* in its proper order—with correct spelling.

Mr. Isaacs also was in charge of the students'

field work, and guided them gently and firmly in becoming the best pastors possible. He insisted they practice all they learned in the classroom. Again, he was tough, and they knew he expected their best. But they knew he was their friend, and they knew they could always rely on his support and love.

By now Lillian had become faculty sponsor for the WMU. She wanted all of the women to see the urgency of missions and was always looking for new talent for the work.

One day she learned that one of the student families, the Faulkenberrys, had lost their 14-year-old son. She went to visit immediately. Lillian listened as Grace Faulkenberry vented her grief. Before she left, however, she asked Grace to be the WMU president. Grace had gained good experience in the First Baptist Church at Pineville, and showed great promise. She became Lillian's helper at home as well as in church, and the two became fast friends. Together they enlisted nearly every woman and child on the campus in WMU organizations. "This is the best organization on the campus and everyone wants to be a member," Grace said often.

Sam Faulkenberry was in John's class in doctrines. Sam had thought he could not memorize the required Scriptures, but John encouraged him. Both were proud of Sam's grades.

One day as Sam studied, he looked up from his Bible and said to Grace, "John Isaacs is the best teacher I've ever had. His humor in the class keeps it alive. But being in there is like sitting at the feet of Jesus. I'd just have to call him a saint."

The two couples shared many holiday occasions, loved each other, and helped each other. They spent so much time together that Johnny began to claim the Faulkenberrys' daughter as his sister.

John continually shared his problems with Lillian just as he had done in Fleming. One day he confided, "My students keep telling me they can't have

Training Union. 'I have to read all the parts,' they say. One student offered a woman a Bible. She said she would take it but she couldn't read it." After a pause John added, "What would you do?"

Lillian answered without having to think about it. "Tell them to teach the people to read."

But that was another problem! How do you teach people—adults—how to read?

Lillian was reminded by God of her calling. She remembered people she had known through the years who could not read. She remembered her own joy in reading. She knew that next to being His child, being able to read was her greatest blessing. She was ready for God to use her.

Unexpectedly, God's plan began to unfold in what seemed to be an insignificant way. The wife of one of the students came to Lillian with a request. She had a recent issue of *Royal Service* in her hand. The issue told about the Laubach Literacy Center at Baylor University in Texas. "Will you order this correspondence course, How to Learn to Teach Adults How to Read?" she asked.

Immediately Lillian filled out the order, and asked about the payment to be enclosed.

"That is why I asked you to fill out the order," the young woman smiled.

"I don't have the money," Lillian answered.

"But the WMU at First Baptist Church in Pineville would pay for it, wouldn't they?" Her insistent question and smile was followed by gracious thanks to Lillian for asking for the money. Then she left.

Lillian did not know what to do. Should she take the request to the WMU? She began to pray. "Lord, do You want me to ask for the money? If You do, help me . . . I believe in Your Word, 'If ye shall ask anything in my name, I will do it' " (John 14:14).

The impression from the Lord was to call Ethel Golden, president of the WMU. Immediately Lillian called her. She received an invitation to speak to

50

the executive committee which would meet at Ethel's house in just a few days.

Lillian continued to pray each day for the Lord to direct her talk to that committee. He assured her He would tell her what to say, and the women would respond. She prayed again as she started to tell them about the woman who could not read her Bible, the students who had to read all the Training Union parts, the people who had to sign an X for their names. Then she told about the Clear Creek woman who wanted the correspondence course.

Lillian was surprised at the question she asked, because she had not planned it. "Ladies, how would you like to take a literacy workshop and learn to teach adults to read and write?"

Sudden silence reigned. No chairs rocked; the porch swing stopped; no fans stirred the air. "What did you say?" came the first startled response.

Lillian barely repeated the question before all of the ladies began to talk at once.

"I don't know anyone who can't read!"

"That's the job of our schools!"

"Why didn't they learn to read when they went to school?"

"They could learn by themselves if they wanted to!"

Lillian showed the defeat she felt as she stood to leave. "Ladies, these people look and act as we do, except they cannot read. They cannot even read God's Word for themselves."

Hot tears stung her eyes and rolled down her cheeks as she drove home. "Lord, I really made a mess of things. Besides, I forgot to ask for money for the correspondence course."

The ringing phone caused her to hurry into the house. Wearily, she answered.

"Forgive me, Lillian! Forgive me!" were the first words she heard.

Since she could not recognize the excited voice, Lillian ventured, "What for?"

Trying to calm her voice, Ethel began to pour out all that had just happened to her. "Lillian, after everybody was gone, Ruth (a 65-year-old woman who ironed for Ethel and others in the WMU) asked me, 'Ethel, when are you going to learn me to read?' I was flabbergasted. I knew she never followed my written instruction to her, but I didn't know she couldn't read. She was ironing on the back porch while we were meeting and heard you ask about the workshop."

Ethel continued hardly catching her breath in her excitement, "I turned to Ruth and said, 'You never told me you couldn't read.' "

"Why should I?" Ruth answered, "You weren't gonna do anything about it. But now after you take the workshop, you can learn me to read!"

By this time, both Ethel and Lillian were shedding tears of joy and relief. Ethel added, "We'll have another meeting at my house next week. Will you forgive me and come to tell us how to have a workshop? I want to teach Ruth to read."

"I will forgive you if you get all the ladies to take the workshop!" Lillian replied with a surge of energy.

"Oh, I will!" Ethel promised.

The Lord directed that next meeting of the executive committee. The ladies could not sit still as they talked. Even the air seemed electrified. Everybody knew Ruth. Mrs. Mary Wilson commanded the attention and respect of all as she spoke, "I move we have the workshop."

"This project is too big for us," someone said.

"We'll have to ask the Bell County Associational WMU to help sponsor it."

The ladies voted, and the motion was carried. Lillian was appointed to explain the need for the workshop and to ask for help at the next associatonal meeting.

The association gladly accepted the challenge, but felt unable financially to bring someone from the Baylor Center to lead it. Again, Lillian was appointed to ask for funding—this time from the Home Mission Board.

Through Dr. A. B. Cash, director of pioneer missions at the Board and a frequent visitor in the Isaacs' home, Lillian learned that the problems and needs for literacy training discovered in Bell County existed everywhere. "Every church in the Southern Baptist Convention needs a reading program," he said. "We need to help people read the Bible with understanding. Go ahead with the project. God will bless it."

At the Mountain Preachers Bible Conference that spring Lillian saw Wendell Belew, director of associational missions for the Home Mission Board. He, too, was a frequent visitor at the Isaacs' home. He shared their dreams for the mountain churches and knew firsthand the needs of the mountain people. She quickly told Dr. Belew about the need for money for a literacy workshop to be held at Clear Creek.

"That's a great idea! You should ask Dr. Rutledge for the money." He introduced Lillian to Dr. Rutledge, director of missions for the Home Mission Board, who was standing nearby.

Dr. Rutledge listened as Lillian again explained the needs. He was thoughtful for a moment. Then he answered, "Just this week at the Board we were exploring new possibilities for meeting the needs of people. Indeed, literacy is a must. Yes, the Home Mission Board will be happy to pay for this project. We will sponsor the workshop."

Now the Bell County Associational WMU women truly were excited. They contacted the Baylor Center for a leader. They planned a rally to inform and promote interest. A publicity committee contacted the county radio stations; a TV station in Knoxville, Tennessee; and newspapers in Pineville and Middlesboro.

"Lillian, you go see the director of the *Middlesboro*

Daily News. Get his support for this project," the committee directed.

Continuously praying that God would go before her, Lillian visited with the sensitive, brilliant, energetic young editor, Ellis Easterly. "Do you want to expand the circulation of your paper?" she asked.

Looking quizzically he responded, "How?"

Thoughtfully answering Lillian said, "By helping adult nonreaders in Bell County and the surrounding area learn to read."

Again he questioned, "How will you do that? Who will pay for the program?"

Quickly Lillian answered, "The Bell County Woman's Missionary Union is planning a literacy workshop to train volunteers to use the Laubach method to teach adults to read. The volunteers will give their time without pay. We're planning to have the workshop at the Clear Creek Baptist School. The Home Mission Board of the Southern Baptist Convention has agreed to pay the expenses for a man to come from Baylor University to conduct the workshop."

The editor was fascinated. In the weeks that followed, he wrote articles to promote literacy. He wondered, "What prompts you and all these Southern Baptists to give their time, energy, and efforts without pay to promote literacy?" It was Lillian's privilege to say, "Because reading is basic in our world and we want every person to be able to read. We want them to read the Bible for themselves."

The editor requested statistics on nonreaders in Bell County. Lillian knew that in the limited time— the rally was set for September 3, 1959—she must go to "the top" for her information.

One morning while praying, Lillian felt impressed to call one of the Kentucky senators in Washington, D. C. When she asked to speak to the senator the secretary blurted, "Is this an emergency? He is in a congressional meeting."

Answering quickly, "Yes, it is an emergency. I need to speak to the senator now."

Then he answered, "Who is it? What can I do for you?"

Enthusiastically Lillian responded, "This is one of your constituents in Bell County. Do you want more people to vote in the next election? I mean people who have become new readers and can read your name and possibly vote for you?"

"Yes, I do!" he flashed.

Then, Lillian explained the literacy project going on in Bell County. Immediately he sent the number of nonreaders in Bell County, Kentucky, and the United States according to the US Bureau of Census in 1950.

The associational WMU worked day and night to promote literacy. Lillian was in the middle of the activity. At home, John ate snacks, or soup from cans, or whatever Lillian prepared for him and Johnny "on the run." One day six-year-old Johnny came in to find his home filled with enthusiastic women and their posters advertising the workshop.

"Literacy, literacy, literacy!" he exclaimed. "I hope everybody in the world learns to read!"

He had expressed the feeling of the women exactly.

October 9-10, 1959, the first literacy workshop sponsored by the Home Mission Board was held at Clear Creek Baptist School. God was in it. More than 200 prospective teachers of literacy came from four states. Included were volunteers from seven counties in Kentucky.

Ellis Easterly wrote an editorial for the October 12 edition of the *Middlesboro Daily News*. "The workshop has been referred to, in an unsophisticated way, as a 'whopping success' by a man who ought to know—Dr. Richard Cortwright, a national authority on literacy who conducted [it]."

Lillian said simply, "God gave the victory."

Ethel began teaching her eager pupil, Ruth Shepherd. Others volunteered to teach persons eager to read.

When the Mountain Preachers Bible Conference met again in Oneida, Kentucky, one year later, the Home Mission Board asked Lillian to give a report on the literacy project. Lillian prayed about what she should say. The answer came clearly. "Take Ruth and let her read My Word and tell what it means to learn to read."

Lillian called Ethel immediately, for Ruth was to work at her house Friday, the day of the report.

Ethel hesitated a moment. "Do you think she'll want to go?"

Lillian answered, "God impressed me to ask her. See what she says."

Ethel stalled, "I need Ruth here to help me."

Then teasing, Lillian said, "Of course, you'll pay her just as if she's working."

Ethel waited no longer. "I'd better see if she wants to go before you charge me for two or three days." Then, there was another pause. "What will she wear?"

Lillian readily answered, "Whatever you provide for her."

Ruth did want to go, and was pleased to be invited. She asked to be allowed to take George, her young teenage grandson, with her.

John and Lillian met Ruth and George on the townsquare early in the day to take them to Oneida. Before they left, Ruth stopped to inspect her new dress in the bank window.

Ruth obviously enjoyed the ride. "Today I'm sittin' and riding' instead of standin' and ironin'—just because I can read," was her first comment. Then she began to read the road signs. Joyfully she spelled and pronounced the words on each of them. "*C-u-r-v-e, curve; s-l-o-w, slow; s-t-o-p, stop.*"

Then she began to reminisce aloud. "I'm the oldest of nine children. The year I started to school, the footlog washed out. My mother said she hoped I could go the next year, but she had a new baby by then and needed me to take care of him.

"Years rolled by. The other children all went on to school, but Mama alway needed me to help tend to the other babies and wash and cook. Finally I got to go to school too, but I was too big and everybody made fun of me—so big a girl and sittin' in the first grade.

"I married early and had babies of my own and I had to work hard—never got done. I'd look at the children's books, like I had looked at my brothers' and sisters' books, and I wanted to read. I couldn't even read the primers.

"But God is good. He heered my prayers. My first big prayer was that God would send a preacher to tell me how to be saved. You know I heered a heap of preachin' before I heered how to be saved."

Lillian interrupted, "Be sure and tell the preachers that today before you read."

Ruth nodded, and adjusted her skirt. Her smile spoke her pleasure in the ride. After a moment or two she took up her reverie, this time with a catch in her voice.

"You remember it was just a year ago when you came to the missionary meet at Ethel's house. You asked the ladies did they want to take a workshop to learn how to teach folks like me to read."

Lillian nodded as Ruth dabbed at her brimming eyes. "Well, the Lord says to me, 'Ruth, that's for you. Listen.' My second big prayer was about to be answered. For years I prayed to learn to read. After I was saved, I prayed to learn to read the Bible."

There was a hush as Ruth told of her experience with Ethel. Then she continued. "You see, I don't rest so good at night. For years my husband and daughter lay sick. I didn't go to bed like other folks. I leaned against the bed to rest when they were both quiet. Then they died, and I took the four grandchildren to raise. George, here, is the young-est. Now at night, when I can't sleep, I remember, 'Ruth, you can read.' I just reach up over my bed and turn on the light. Some nights I read till 2:00 in the morning. But what would you do if you had never read this Book? Now, my third prayer is that God will let me read this Book from kiver to kiver."

By now the car had pulled up to the meeting place. Lillian turned to Ruth and suggested, "Ruth, share what learning to read means to you. Then read your favorite chapter."

Ruth agreed, and smiled as she said, "I'll read part of the third chapter of John."

The time came for Ruth to speak on the program. She straightened her skirt with a quick brush of her hand. She stood erect and held her head up. "I thank God that I have learned to read. I thank Him for Ethel who taught me. I thank Him for the day Mrs. Isaacs asked the ladies to take a workshop. There are other folks like me who want to learn to read. There is nothing like readin'. Next to being saved, it's the greatest thing that ever happened to me."

Then Ruth shared some of the testimony she had given as she rode with the Isaacs to the meeting.

Many eyes filled with tears as Ruth concluded. "Reading makes shoppin' easy. I can read the la-bels, read my mail, read the street signs, read the newspaper. Most of all I can read my Bible. Now I will read part of my favorite chapter, John 3."

When she got to the word *condemnation* Ruth spelled and sounded it out. "*C-o-n-, con; d-e-m, dem; n-a-t-i-o-n, nation*. That *condemnation* word gives me a little trouble, but I know what it means.

"Are you thankful you can read?" Ruth asked.

There was a profound stillness in the auditorium. Only the sound of throats being cleared and noses being blown broke the silence.

A noted preacher was programmed to follow

Ruth. He said nothing for a long moment. Carefully, as though not trusting his voice, he began. He declared that he had never heard a more eloquent reading of the Scriptures or testimony to their message. "I've not been moved in this way since the day of my own salvation," he said.

Quietly he made a few remarks saying that no further sermon was necessary. The meeting was adjourned.

John and Lillian, Ruth and George were guests in the dining room for lunch. Delicious food was passed around the table but Ruth's plate remained empty. Lillian became concerned. "Ruth, take some of this good food."

"No, I can't eat," came the reply.

"Aren't you hungry?" Lillian wanted to know.

Ruth nodded. "Yes, but I can't eat today. This is the first time in my life I'm being waited on at the table instead of doin' the waitin' on just because I can read."

With a smile, she continued. "It is a sacred hour. Do you remember readin' in the Bible about David longin' for a drink of water from that well at Bethlehem (1 Chron. 11:11-19)? Three soldiers broke through the Philistines' army to get David a drink. Did he drink it?"

Lillian shook her head, "No."

Ruth continued, "David poured out the water to the Lord. It was holy because those fellers risked their lives to get it. This is a holy hour. I offer it to God because I have learned to read."

The next day Lillian talked with Ellis Easterly, editor of the *Middlesboro Daily News*, about Ruth's experience. Ellis turned toward the window and moved to adjust the shade. When he had full control of the shake in his voice, he asked for a picture of Ruth for the front of the next day's paper. His article gave a needed boost to the literacy work. The teachers stayed busy.

John and Lillian were interested in the brilliant

young editor. They continued to pray for Ellis, even after they left Kentucky. Years later they heard that God had saved him and called him to preach. His degrees in journalism laid aside, he went to Clear Creek Baptist School for a year to learn the Bible. Then he attended New Orleans Baptist Theological Seminary to take a doctorate in Archeology.

John and Lillian Isaacs were not the only persons at Clear Creek to promote literacy. The president and his wife, Dr. and Mrs. D. M. Aldridge, encouraged the movement. Many of John's students and others attended the literacy workshop and began teaching. Others, like Grace Faulkenberry, gave "wheels" to whomever needed to be transported to teach or to learn. The WMU supported with prayer and enlisted others to do the same.

The days at Clear Creek were fulfilling to both John and Lillian. Each of them had found a real place of service. They were happy where God had placed them. As always, both arose each morning thrilled about what God was going to do in their lives on that day.

6
Call to Be Pioneers

"LOOK, Mother, He's done it again!" he exclaimed as he looked out of his window at the sun splashed mountainside.

"Who's done what, Johnny?" queried Lillian.

"He's made another day! What are we going to do today?"

Indeed it seemed that God did make every day beautiful for the Isaacs, and they saw His presence in each part of it. He was making a new adventure for them that would be unique and filled with places and people they could only imagine. It all started with a ringing phone.

John laid down his evening paper. "I'll get it," he said, and gave a chipper hello to the waiting caller.

"Yes." Pause. "We're fine, thank you," John answered. Lillian continued to read.

"I'm going to ask you a question, John. Now don't say no until you have prayed about it," came the strange statement from their friend, Dr. A. B. Cash of the Home Mission Board.

"Oh, I won't answer without praying," John assured him.

"How would you (and Lillian) like to go to Fairbanks, Alaska, to be pastor of Native Baptist Mission?"

John said nothing, but his thoughts spun crazily. "It's so cold there! I thought only Eskimos could really survive that weather! It's so far away! So cold! So cold!"

Lillian looked up to see her husband staring at the wall. Dr. Cash, alarmed by the long silence, shouted into the phone, "John, are you still there? Let me speak to Lillian."

Without a word John handed the phone to Lillian. She was puzzled by the sober expression on John's face, but happily said, "Hello."

"Lillian, how would you like to go to Alaska?" Dr. Cash asked again.

Lillian recognized her friend's voice. "Why, I'd love to go. When?" was her instant reply.

They talked a short time before she asked, "Why did you ask us?"

"Well," Dr. Cash recalled, "I have just gotten back from Alaska myself. I walked the streets of Fairbanks at midnight on June 21 while it was light all night. As I walked I asked the Lord who should come and work at the mission. It was as though a voice spoke clearly, 'John and Lillian Isaacs.' I walked a little further, and then I prayed again. 'Excuse me, Lord, I am going to ask you again.' And again the voice said, 'John and Lillian Isaacs.' "

With confidence, Lillian then concluded, "If the Lord told you that, then I expect we will go. When John Isaacs prays, he finds what the Lord wants him to do."

John was silent for many days. In the meantime, Lillian had many questions. "Will we move our 'junk'?" she wondered, thinking that she would not mind moving anywhere if she did not have to pack up everything in the house and take it with her. "How will we ever move all of John's books?

I know he'll want every one of them. How will we heat our house? Will we have coal stoves like the ones we had in Fleming?" But she was not worried. She was, in fact, ecstatically happy. "If it's God's will we go; if it's God's will we stay."

Finally John was ready with an answer. "I cannot find any reason for not going to Alaska except a selfish one. I remember the verse that says, 'For I will shew him how great things he must suffer for my name's sake' (Acts 9:16 KJV). I am so ashamed that I have never suffered anything for Jesus. So it looks like we are going."

They met with Dr. Cash almost immediately. He gave them information about which household goods to take, what to store, and what to buy immediately when they arrived. Dr. Cash gave them instructions for their work as well. "I think you will find the literacy ministry helpful in your work there. But go, and see what God wants you to do. Then, just do whatever needs to be done."

John and Lillian look at a map before leaving for Alaska (1960).

Snowtracks
(1960-1972)

7
The Trip

THE trip to Alaska was something to remember. The Isaacs sold their furniture and loaded their other belongings, including all of John's books, into a small trailer hitched to their old Ford. Then they set out on a two-week adventure. They drove all day and stopped late each afternoon for dinner, sight-seeing, and rest. The next morning, after Lillian packed a picnic lunch, they set out again. They drove by Yellowstone National Park, through Wyoming and Montana. Johnny was entertained by the games they played as they moved toward the Alcan Highway and by the stories shared by his parents.

John told Johnny of Civil War days, when John Isaacs XIII, Johnny's paternal grandfather, was a boy. Too small to shoot a gun, the boy loaded muskets. He assisted Confederate soldiers who fired on the Yankees from the attic windows of his home. John remembered too that his paternal grandfather was originally from Holland and spoke Dutch. Johnny was fascinated. John told of the beautiful Christmas parties in his maternal grandparents' home near Pores Knob, North Carolina, and of the summer picnics on the back porch that overlooked a whole range of mountains. He told of the school that met in his home and how the teacher, his father, had been a stalwart Christian guide for the students. What pictures of both excitement and peace he painted with his words!

"And when I was just your age, I killed a diamondback rattler—as big as my arm— in our pasture. I had to do it to protect my sister!"

"I would run from any snake, Daddy," Johnny said as he measured John's arm for size. "Will there be snakes in Alaska?"

"You won't have to worry," John assured him. "But maybe we'll see some bears."

"That's OK. I like bears better!" Johnny thought a minute of future adventures. Then he turned to Lillian.

"Mother, tell about when you were a little girl," he begged.

"Well, there was the time I decided to fly," Lillian said trying to change the subject from both snakes and bears. "I used my mother's big black umbrella for my airplane and took several trips from the fence into the pasture. But my plane cracked up on the last jump, and I was terrified. I knew my mother would be upset. I folded the bent and broken ribs carefully and returned the big black umbrella to its container. I decided to wait until it rained again to find out just how upset she would be."

Johnny, wide-eyed, asked, "Was she upset, Mama?"

"Oh, yes! And she showed me how much—with a switch."

"Tell me some more," Johnny encouraged.

"Oh, I remember going to Sunday School— sometimes at the Baptist church and sometimes at the Methodist church. When I was in the card class for preschoolers I could already read all of the Bible verses on the cards. The Bible came to be my favorite book. I found that when I read it, Jesus talked to me. He was my friend. I'd find verses that seemed to fit my needs perfectly. My favorite was, and still is, "And thine ears shall hear a word behind thee, saying, This is the way, walk ye in it, when ye turn to the right hand, and when ye turn to the left" (Isa. 30:21 KJV).

Then Lillian told of studying the "eleventh commandment" in Matthew 22:36-39 when she was still a preschooler. After a moment of thought, she asked her teacher, "What are the other ten commandments, and where are they?"

The teacher and the Sunday School superintendent cleared their throats and tried to skip by the little girl's question. Instead of forgetting about it, Lillian searched in her own Bible at home until she found the missing commandments.

On the following Sunday, during opening assembly, the superintendent called for announcements. A tiny head bobbed just above the pewbacks. And a strong voice spoke out, "I want to announce that the ten commandments are found in Exodus, twentieth chapter."

Lillian laughed as she concluded. "There was a long silence and then assembly was dismissed." John and Johnny laughed too.

This kind of story provided a perfect lead into quoting verses or telling Bible stories or other stories from childhood.

"Mama, how do you know so many stories?"

"Johnny, I listened to a lot of stories as I grew up. And I can't remember when I couldn't read. I read every book I could get my hands on—fairy tales, novels, schoolbooks, encyclopedias, and especially the Bible. Once I had a strange experience while I was reading. My father and several other men were reloading cotton bales from our wagon. You know, I could pick a big bag of cotton in a day when I was your age. My father would have me weigh the cotton and figure how much money I'd made. Then I added those pounds and pennies to the running total. One summer I picked a thousand pounds—a whole bale.

"Well, on this particular day, there was one more bale on the wagon. One of the men said, 'Y'all can go on, I'll just push this one off the wagon, and we'll get it later.' He pushed and pushed but the bale wouldn't budge. Finally he called for help. His friends teased him. They came back and all struggled with the bale. It just would not move. Finally, my father came. Even his added strength couldn't make the bale move one inch. Father was perplexed. He jumped from the wagon and began to investigate this strange bale of cotton.

"There I sat with my book, beside the wagon, unaware of any danger.

" 'Move, Lillian,' my father shouted. And I did!

"Then, with one hand my father pushed the bale off the wagon. It landed in the exact spot where I had been sitting only seconds before. Johnny, an angel kept that bale from falling on me."

"Looks like we need to stop here at Great Falls (Montana), Johnny," John broke into the fun. "We're about to go into Canada. We'll pack everything from the trailer into boxes and ship it from here." After two days of repacking and shipping, the three moved on. Through Canada and Alaska, they made their way. Finally they drove into Fairbanks, finishing their more than 5,000-mile trip.

The Isaacs pulled up to their new home on the corner of Fifteenth and Lacey Streets. Johnny was out of the car almost before it stopped. He raced toward a little boy he had seen playing across the street. John took in the whole scene in a glance before walking across Lacey Street to examine the outside of Native Baptist Mission. Lillian went to the house. She was thrilled to find it furnished by the Home Mission Board through the Annie Armstrong Easter Offering. She saw there would be little trouble fitting their few belongings into their new house. She checked on Johnny, happily playing with his new friend, Joe, then joined John at the mission.

They entered at the front door on Lacey, saw the sanctuary, and walked toward the pulpit. John tried out the steps, the chairs, and the pulpit. He opened the pulpit Bible and pictured himself preaching to an expectant congregation.

They looked at the Sunday School rooms behind the sanctuary and then went downstairs to see the kitchen, more Sunday School rooms, and the large fellowship hall. Lillian pictured the rooms full of smiling faces reading God's Word. They anticipated their work with excitement and an abounding joy that only God could give.

A few days of exploring by foot and a few shopping trips by car gave them a feel for their new community. They drove down Cushman, the main street in this town of about 12,000. Most streets crossing Cushman were narrow and unpaved. There were few sidewalks and many log houses. Most of the grocery and department stores in town were locally owned and small, except for one new, large supermarket. They located the school Johnny would attend in just a few days. They were pleased to learn that the Fairbanks school system was one of the highest rated school systems in the country.

The Isaacs spoke to everyone they saw. Instantly they loved these friendly people. They found the residents eager to help them get acquainted with the city.

Immediately they felt accepted. They were at home!

8
Beginnings

THE Isaacs knew before coming to Alaska that the Native Baptist Mission building was being used temporarily by people of First Baptist Church of Fairbanks. The old First Baptist building had burned. Until their own building was ready, the two congregations would meet together. The pastor of First Baptist Church continued to preach while John began to drive the mission bus to transport children and adults for Sunday School and worship.

John and Lillian soon learned that the people in Fairbanks liked to arrive at church early. Those who did not ride the bus came even earlier than those who did. They arrived by 8:00 A.M. and seemed eager to start services immediately. Since John had already gone on the bus route, Lillian and Johnny began to meet the early arrivals at the church. They learned Scripture verses and sang, and Lillian told Bible stories.

The Isaacs met Tom and Elsie Willock their first week in Alaska. They were the first Eskimo Baptists, and Uncle Tom was the first Eskimo deacon. They were baptized into the First Baptist Church of Fairbanks in 1947 and were charter members of Native Baptist Mission. Dr. Cash had told the Isaacs much about the Willocks' early life. Uncle Tom and Aunt Elsie added colorful facts and details.

Aunt Elsie was born in 1887 in the cold of December above the Arctic Circle. Before Elsie's birth, her mother built a little hut of branches lined with moss and leaves. The birth took place there, outside of the regular living quarters. Only old clothing was worn to the birth shelter, for everything used must be burned before the mother and new baby could return. "If this baby is a girl, just put dirt in its mouth," an older resident in the village instructed. But Elsie's mother wanted her baby even if it were a girl. So, Elsie lived.

She and Uncle Tom came from families that herded reindeer. Later, they were asked to leave the village because Tom was sick. They took their children and as much provisions as the sled would hold and left. It was the worst of winter. God helped them find an old cabin where they clung to life. When the last of the flour was gone, they prayed lying facedown on the dirt floor, and asked for help to keep them from starving.

Elsie felt impressed to make a snare for birds although this was not the season for birds. On the first day, they caught one bird; on the second, two; the third, three. They were filled and satisfied. The birds continued to be supplied, at last in such numbers that the Willocks took many back to their friends in the village.

The Isaacs learned that the Alaskan people arrived at church early. They also learned that most of the children were not "church-broke." They loved to play in the sanctuary—running, rolling under the pews, or leaping over them. No one had taught them to sit through the service without leaving and returning several times. The lack of a worshipful atmosphere bothered the new missionaries. Their first Sunday afternoon in Alaska the Isaacs

73

prayed that God would show them how to minister to these people.

God seemed to answer them immediately. "Teach them My Word. I will take care of the rest."

As John and Lillian continued to pray about ways to minister, they learned that many of the adults could not read. If they were to teach the Word, they would need to teach nonreaders how to read the Bible for themselves. The Holy Spirit impressed them to talk with the Tanana Valley Associational Woman's Missionary Union about a literacy workshop similar to the one Lillian had spearheaded in Kentucky. The WMU was thrilled to help in any way. With the Isaacs leading, and the associational WMU sponsoring, ten people completed the workshop.

Immediately after the workshop, Lillian asked Aunt Elsie if she would like to learn to read better so she could read her Bible. Aunt Elsie explained, "I can read readin' some, but I can't read writin' or write writin'. Tom can't read readin' or write writin', either one. But we want to read the Bible."

They set a time to begin lessons. Uncle Tom and Aunt Elsie came eagerly to the Isaacs' home and brought others with them. Sometimes as many as 11 came. Those who could not read anything went into the living room with Uncle Tom and Lillian. They started with the Laubach system. Those who could read a little stayed around the kitchen table with Aunt Elsie and John. They studied more difficult words. All studied the Bible, following with a finger as John or Lillian read. Usually, John explained the passage.

Each session started with the students telling something wonderful God had done for them. Each night they sang and prayed. And they always had refreshments. They loved the classes and wanted to meet often. By October the Isaacs had started a literacy school. Classes for two levels met four times each week.

Both Aunt Elsie and Uncle Tom had trouble seeing the printed page. He could still see well enough to shoot squirrels from a tree, but she was unable to sew the decorative beaded garments she once made. The Isaacs made appointments for both Uncle Tom and Aunt Elsie to have eye examinations. The Lions Club bought their glasses. Now both could learn to read the Bible. The thrill of reading was as great for these senior adults (at 83 and 76) as it is for any first-grader.

Tom learned the word *fish* first. His new glasses allowed him to make gill nets to string across the river. In this way he could catch enough of the big fish to provide his winter meat. The word *fish* related to his life.

Then, when he learned the word *Jesus* he wept openly. "Let me look at that name again—the name above every name. I thought sure I would die and go to heaven and never know His name. If only the missionaries had learned me to read 50 years ago, I could have been a greater blessing to my people. But God let my dream come true. He let me learn to read His Word."

Happy days went by quickly. Often Aunt Elsie came to see her good friend Lillian between classes. One cold winter day as they talked and drank tea, Aunt Elsie confided she wanted to tell Lillian something, but felt hesitant. Lillian was always receptive. She quietly leaned closer, placed her hand on the browned arm of her friend and said, "Aunt Elsie, you can tell me anything."

"I can?"

"Sure," replied Lillian.

"I want to take a bubble bath," Aunt Elsie grinned childlike.

"Of course you do. One of these days, you . . ."

"No, today!" interrupted Aunt Elsie.

"Oh," Lillian looked up startled, but quickly regained her composure. "Of course, today! Come right on back to the bathroom, and we'll get everything ready."

Lillian poured the rich bubbly oil into hot running water. She took out her two warmest, fluffiest, prettiest towels and bathcloths. "These are for you to use, Aunt Elsie. Make yourself at home. I'll have fresh tea for you when you finish."

"Oh, so-o-o soft, so-o-o pretty, smell so-o-o good," murmured Aunt Elsie as she buried her face in the pink softness of the bathcloth and made ready for her first bubble bath.

Tom took seriously the sermons and teachings he heard at church. When he learned about tithing, he believed he should tithe.

One Saturday afternoon, Tom came into the church and laid some money on the top of the piano where Alma Dunkin, a volunteer missionary, was playing.

"What is this, Tom? What are you doing?"

Tom replied simply, "Tithing."

"Oh," Alma explained, "you can bring your tithe tomorrow and put it in the offering plate."

"But I got paid today," Tom stated.

Picking up the bills, Alma counted them. "Ten, 20, 30, 40, . . . 90. How much money did you make this week?"

"One-hundred dollars," Tom answered.

Surprised, Alma explained further. "Ten dollars is a tithe of $100. Any more is an offering."

Now Tom was the one surprised. "You must be mistaken! Jesus died for me. Surely I should give him $90 and keep $10 for me."

Alma explained again, and finally Tom was content to leave his tithe and an offering. Taking the rest of the money, he said, "I'll go now and buy grub."

Tom was full of gratitude for Jesus. He was grateful too for those who told him of Jesus. After he learned to write, he wrote a letter to Dr. A. B. Cash to thank the Home Mission Board for sending missionaries to Alaska. The only other letter he ever wrote was to Alma and C. O. Dunkin, volunteer missionaries, thanking them for telling him about Jesus.

Elsie too learned to write well enough to write a letter to her sister Frieda in Kotzebue, Alaska. Frieda took the letter to a missionary in Kotzebue to read for her. When Frieda learned that Elsie could read and write, she wanted to learn for herself and asked the missionary to teach her.

Elsie remained excited about her increased ability to read. "The greatest blessing I ever had was hearing about Jesus and believing in him as my Saviour. My second greatest blessing is learning to read His Word and hearing Him talk to me."

Six-year-old Johnny loved his new home in Alaska and enjoyed playing with his new friend Joe Plutt. They went to school together and shared many little-boy games and secrets. One day both boys brought home papers asking their parents for certain information.

"My mama can't read these papers," Joe remarked matter-of-factly.

"My mama can read anything! Bring them to my house," Johnny invited.

Joe did bring his papers, along with his mother and his brother and sister. Together, they struggled to get the information. Lillian would ask Joe the question and he would translate into the Slavic language of his mother. After she told him the answer, he would translate into English. Lillian would write and start the process again. When the paper was finished, Lillian smiled at Mary Plutt. She loved this beautiful young Yugoslavian neighbor.

"Mary, would you like to learn English?"

Mary's bright smile gave her answer before she exclaimed, "Yes! Yes!"

"When do your little ones take a nap?" asked Lillian.

"Whenever you teach me," Mary replied.

They arranged immediately for Lillian to go to

Mary's house four mornings each week to teach English as a second language. Mary Plutt told her friends in the Yugoslav community, and found others who wanted to learn.

Word spread quickly among the foreign born. Lillian called Liz Hall, who had completed the workshop, to help. With her Swiss background, linguistic ability, and love for people, Liz was perfect for teaching the foreign born. In a short time Lillian and Liz were teaching in 13 different homes, mornings and afternoons, five days each week.

Six weeks after the Isaacs got to Fairbanks, the First Baptist Church moved into its new building. John took over preaching responsibilities at Native Baptist Mission. His first Sunday was full of surprises.

John drove the bus, as usual, to gather his flock. Then he taught his Sunday School class. As the worship hour approached, he remembered with joy the message of God's love he was bringing. He also remembered other first sermons—at Neon, at Fleming, at the little church during seminary days.

He read his Scripture selection and gave an introduction. Without the First Baptist congregation the group seemed small—and so restless. Never had he been so aware of both children and adults coming and going all through the service. Finally, he came to the climax of the sermon. All was unusually quiet as he gave the invitation and announced a hymn. The congregation stood to sing. As they sang, three people walked to the front.

The excited pastor greeted each one and waited for each to tell what response he was making to the invitation. The first said, "I want to ride on the front seat of the bus going home today." The second said, "I want to go to the bathroom. Which way?" The third said, "I just wanted to know what you say to people who come and shake your hand."

In desperation John bowed his head as he said quietly, "Let us pray."

78

All seemed to go wrong that day. John drove through the complete bus route but still had several passengers. "Didn't I pass your home back a ways?" he asked one of the children. When the child gave a "yes" grunt, John asked, "Why didn't you tell me to stop so you could get off?"

"Oh," the child replied, wide-eyed, "I like to ride the bus. I knew you would take me by again."

Finally John delivered all of his passengers to their homes. He pulled his coat around his neck as he felt the chill of October from the opening of the door. He also felt a twinge of wonder at all that must be done with these dear people. "Lord," he prayed, "I know You brought us here. Show us what to do and how, so we may give glory to Your name in this place. Amen." With a touch of humor returned, he added, "And, Lord, help me learn this bus route pretty quick!"

John started a Thursday morning Bible study group his first week in Fairbanks. One person John enlisted was Gracie. Gracie had several children and many problems. She learned early that John and Lillian were good listeners and she visited them often. They prayed with her, read the Bible with her, and gave her memory verses to learn. They told Gracie about the Bible study. Gracie came and enjoyed it. She learned God's word and grew to depend on God for strength.

Another faithful Eskimo member of the group was Ella. She and her Anglo husband Irvin; their son Johnny; and their beautiful German shepherd, Champ, lived down the street from the Isaacs. Ella was a nonattending member of the mission. She worked at the army post. Irv owned a liquor store and was not a church member anywhere. Champ roamed the neighborhood. He could often be found at the Isaacs' house. It was his custom to bark until John went outside to play with him. He usually brought his own ball. Occasionally, Champ would come and bark when John was not at home or too busy to go out to play. In that case, Lillian would go to the door and talk with the friendly dog. "John can't come out to play now, Champ. He's busy. Just run on home and come another time." Lillian insisted that Champ smiled at her as he picked up his ball and ran toward home.

Lillian and John kept inviting Ella and Irv to the services at the mission, but their words seemed to be wasted. Then one day Ella became ill. Lillian visited her regularly. She took soup, fruit, or other food, and Scripture cards. At times John went also. Both prayed for her.

When Ella got well, she began to come to worship services at the mission and to the Bible study. She learned about tithing from the Bible study and began to practice it. Ella always requested prayer for Irv. She knew he was not well. When the Isaacs visited, Irv remained aloof. John would say, "Irv, you are sick. Won't you turn your life over to Jesus?" The answer remained, "No," and Ella continued to pray. (The Isaacs had been gone from Alaska for some eight years when the prayers for Irv were answered.)

John and Lillian were faithful in their new ministry. In spite of their hard work, almost a year passed before anyone made a profession of faith in Jesus. John and Lillian had visited and prayed, had taught Bible studies and English classes, had ministered in hospitals and homes, and had witnessed faithfully. One Sunday morning John stood up to preach. By now there were no more surprises for John, or so he thought. As usual, he poured out his heart, telling of God's love to His people. He gave the invitation to come to Jesus. Eagerly his eyes skimmed the congregation as he tried to detect some movement or indication of interest. Suddenly, John looked down and noticed seven-year-old Johnny standing at his side. "Johnny, what are you doing up here?" he asked, wondering how the boy had managed to slip away from Lillian.

80

"Daddy, I want to accept Jesus as my Saviour. I want to ask him into my heart."

John's surprise changed to overwhelming joy! His own son was his first convert in Alaska.

Alaska's 24 hours of summer sunlight was still new to the Isaacs in July of 1961. Learning to sleep in the continuous light was difficult, but tightly-closed blinds helped. One morning at 2:30 Lillian heard a loud knock at the door. She pulled on a robe and, trying to keep her eyes open, made her way to the back door.

There stood Aunt Elsie. "Come in, come in, Aunt Elsie. Can I help you? Is something wrong? Would you like a cup of coffee?"

"I want to read God's Word and pray," Aunt Elsie said quietly.

Lillian got her Bible and opened it to the Psalms. After they had read several of them, Elsie said, "Read about heaven."

Lillian turned to John 14 and read aloud again for a while.

"Let's pray," Aunt Elsie said. As they bowed their heads, Aunt Elsie began to pray in Eskimo. She praised God for all his goodness to her and her family. She thanked Him for salvation and for heaven and for good people like the Isaacs who came to tell people about Jesus. When she had finished praying, she said, "Tom gone to live with Jesus."

"Oh," said Lillian quietly, "did Tom die?"

"No, him not dead," Aunt Elsie said triumphantly. "Him gone to live with Jesus. Tom a Christian. Him never die. Seven angels come take him soul away."

"What happened, Aunt Elsie?" Lillian rephrased the question as she prepared coffee for both of them.

Aunt Elsie then told how they had been at the fish camp on the river. Tom was picking the gill nets he had strung across the river. He would throw the fish up on the bank where Elsie would clean and cut them with her *ulu* to dry for the coming winter. Two grandchildren were with her. Suddenly she heard Tom cry out, "Oh, Elsie, my heart, my heart."

While she held the children's hands and watched him, he said, "Never mind, Elsie, I see seven angels on the water (she held up seven fingers just as he had done) coming to take me to heaven."

"Me stood straight and sing Tom's favorite hymn. Sing all the verses as seven angels (she held up seven fingers again) take him soul away to live with Jesus."

About that time someone from a nearby camp came over. "Oh, look at Tom! What's the matter with him? He look like he dead."

"Tom never die," Elsie affirmed. "Seven angels take him soul to live with Jesus. You go get Tom's body and bring it to shore. But Tom not dead."

"Here, Elsie," the neighbor said, taking a bottle of whiskey from his hip pocket, "take a drink and brace yourself in the hour of death."

"Get thee behind me, Satan," Elsie said. "Me have Jesus in my heart. No need drink!"

Elsie had come immediately to the Isaacs to read the Word and pray. "Now," she added after the important things were done, "me go home to bath and sleep. John Isaacs go get Tom's body to bury."

Lillian waked John and told him what had happened. She prepared breakfast for him, knowing he would be gone until lunchtime or later making funeral arrangements and visiting with Uncle Tom's family.

Then Lillian poured herself another cup of coffee and sat at the kitchen table to think, read the Word, and pray. She remembered the exciting times around that table when Aunt Elsie and Uncle Tom shared the goodness of God. They never would start a class without telling something good God had done.

Lillian remembered the program, "This Is Your Life, Uncle Tom Willock," which had been given at the mission just a few weeks before. The president of the Alaska Baptist Convention, Dr. A. B. Cash of the Home Mission Board, Louise Yarbrough of the WMU of Alaska, pastors of churches in the association, and many others had gathered to honor Uncle Tom. Lillian thanked God they had not waited too late. Then she thanked God for Uncle Tom and Aunt Elsie. This time was one of thanksgiving, praise, and preparation for all that must be done.

Aunt Elsie wanted Tom to have a Christian funeral. John and Lillian agreed. They felt it provided a wonderful opportunity for teaching what Christians believe about death. Everybody in Fairbanks loved and respected Tom Willock. Most of the people at the mission could talk of nothing but his death. His was to be the first Christian funeral most of them had ever witnessed.

Since none of the children or adults knew what behavior was expected, and since Eskimo customs were quite different, and since many foreign-born Christians and non-Christians would be in attendance, specific instructions were given at church on Sunday before the funeral.

"Sit quietly and pray," Lillian said. "No chewing gum, no talking or whispering, no going in and out to the bathroom or to get water, no peeking into the box where Tom's body is resting. Sing with the others. Listen to the preacher when he speaks. Speak softly and kindly to Aunt Elsie and their children. Pray."

Many questions were asked about the box that held Uncle Tom's body, the men who brought it into the church, Uncle Tom's home in heaven, and his Saviour who took him there. The funeral was a time for praise to God. Many Christians gave testimonies, and John preached a simple gospel message. Aunt Elsie sang, "In the Sweet By and

83

By," Uncle Tom's favorite hymn. Her faith was strong.

Those who came to the funeral experienced the presence of Tom's God, even as they honored their beloved friend who had gone to live in his heavenly home.

Lillian talks with Aunt Elsie Willock, the first Eskimo Baptist.

9
Expansion

VISITING prospects was important to John and Lillian and their co-workers in Alaska. Liz Hall was a great help in this area as well as in teaching. As she heard names of prospects she would get addresses so she could visit. Liz was so eager that one day when the temperature was 60 degrees below zero, she knocked at Lillian's door ready to go visiting. "Let's see if we can find some others to teach today," she said.

"Oh, yes," was Lillian's reply. "Come in and we'll have our prayer here before we go. It's too cold to sit in the car today even to pray." Together they asked God to lead them to some person in need. They started out to see a Japanese lady whose address they had secured. Liz and Lillian knocked and were invited in. Inside they found five Japanese women playing cards. In Alaska, visitors are always asked inside. Today, however, they were not offered a seat.

"Why you visit in such bad weather?" the woman wanted to know immediately.

"We came from Native Baptist Mission," Lillian explained. "We are trying to find people who would like to learn to speak and write English."

The card playing stopped at once, and the hostess said, "Have a seat. We glad to see you. We interested in English. When we start?"

After a brief moment of questions and answers, Lillian and Liz were invited to come the next day to start an English class. They made sure they knew the correct address and the correct time—9:00 A.M..

That night the temperature dropped even lower. The thermometer registered 66 degrees below zero. All four tires on Liz's car were flat. Only two tires were flat on the Isaacs' car, but John said, "It's too cold to get out. Surely they won't be looking for you."

"But we ought to go," insisted Lillian. "They are expecting us."

John stood firm. "I couldn't get two tires ready before 9:00. They will understand. It's too cold."

At intervals during the morning the conversation returned to going to teach the Japanese women. "What about a taxi?" Lillian was saying as the phone rang.

"I Mayko. Where you?"

"I'm at home," replied Lillian.

"Why you not come?"

"It's 66 degrees below zero."

"I not ask temperature. I say, why you not come?"

"It is so cold the tires went flat."

"I not ask that. I walk one mile to get to begin English lesson, and you not come."

Lillian felt rebuked! She made a personal commitment at that moment that somehow she would meet every appointment with a foreign-born person. "It's so important not to disappoint them," she said.

After much encouraging and persuasion, another time was set to start Mayko's lessons. When Lillian went to her house, her hostess closed the door and locked it. She said, "You see, if someone come to my door, I not home. I study English."

Then she served Lillian tea and cookies. Mayko only drank tea. They started lessons and set a regular time for them to continue. Each time, Mayko served tea and cookies, though she only drank tea.

One day, after Mayko felt confidence in her teacher, she said, "You see, I never touch cookies."

"Yes, Mayko, I noticed that. Don't you like cookies?" Lillian inquired.

"Yes, but I cannot swallow cookies—stick in throat." Then Mayko poured out a story that was almost unbelievable. When she was a child she was taken to live with her grandmother. At a young age, she became a servant for her grandmother and was forced to work hard keeping house and cooking. One day she took a cookie from her grandmother's box. The cookies were counted. Mayko was called a thief, beaten severely, and made to sleep in a tree. That night the temperature dropped and Mayko shivered with cold and fear. The next day she begged her grandmother to forgive her and let her work in the house once more.

Mayko continued, "My grandmother tried to sell me to a circus, but they say I too ugly. So she put me work in rice fields. My leg hurt and began to swell to size of my body. I cry but had to keep working. Finally I cry, 'O God out there, wherever you are, help me. I have such pain! Buddha does not hear me. There must be a God in this world somewhere who love a little girl! Help me!' Strange warm feeling move over body—all through the swell up leg. Leg was well. I work, not hurt anywhere. And I remember there a God somewhere who love a little girl. I not know His name or anything about Him except He love me."

Two unfinished cookies lay in Lillian's plate. Her tea got cold, and a tear rolled down her cheek as she listened to Mayko. But the young woman was not finished. "Another time I have ear infection. When I sleep on my mat on floor I cry without sound because I was not allowed to make noise. Then I remember God who love me and made leg well. I pray in whisper, 'God out there wherever You are, You made my leg well. My ear killing me. I know You can touch it and make me well, so help me. I don't know Your name, but help me.' Same warm feeling come over me again. Ear well."

"Then when you come to teach me and tell me about Jesus—when you say His name—same warm feeling come over me again. God who heard me and made me well was Jesus. I want to know more about Him."

Lillian was thrilled to invite Mayko to church where she could find out more about Jesus, the God who loved her. She was faithful in attendance. One day she said to Lillian, "I believe in prayer, and I believe in Jesus. I really trust Him if He would only help me."

"What do you need?" Lillian asked. She wondered what could bother her friend so much.

"I need citizenship. I can never be citizen."

"Why not?" Lillian wanted to know.

"I live with grandmother till I 12 years old. Then I put out of house for good. Went far away . . . learned to cut hair . . . meet American soldier. He bring to California, took to apartment, then disappear. I almost starve. Not know language. Had no food. Landlord come and knock on door, I not answer. I afraid. Finally landlord decide GI had left. She unlock door; found me almost dead. She brought me back to life. She feed me and care for me. I know how to work, so I work for her.

"Then I become migrant. Went up and down coast to help gather crops. Then I become prostitute—easier than picking crops. But when I apply for citizenship, someone put on record about being prostitute. Immigration officer look at application and say I never be American citizen. I left.

"You see, I nobody. I have no country. Husband desert me. I was prostitute. Finally I marry again, and he brought me to Alaska. If your Jesus can help me become citizen, then I know He can answer every prayer."

"Mayko," Lillian said, for she was moved by the story, "why don't you pray about the matter?"

"I do, I do," Mayko replied quickly, "but I want *you* to pray too."

"I will pray about it, and I will go to see the immigration officer," Lillian promised. Then she continued the lesson for the day. At home John joined her in prayer for Mayko. As soon as possible she made an appointment with the immigration officer.

"What can I do for you today, Mrs. Isaacs?" the officer greeted her warmly.

"I want to tell you a story," Lillian replied and began to tell about Mayko. When she had finished the story, the officer said, "Just a minute. Let me check my files."

He went to the record file, half turning his back to Lillian. She could see he was wiping the tears from his eyes. She whispered, "Thank you, Lord. I know he has heard."

The officer returned and cleared his throat. "Take this application form to Mayko and have her fill it out. It seems her file has been misplaced."

"Thank you," Lillian smiled broadly. "I certainly will."

"See that she gets it done right away," he added as he escorted Lillian to the door.

When Mayko finished studying for citizenship she went to take the test. She did not miss a single question. The officer was impressed with her knowledge and appearance. Later he told the Isaacs, "If I did not know about the Christian religion, I would become a believer because of the transformation I have seen in the life of Mayko. She has hope instead of despair; she is attractive instead of unattractive; she has purpose in her life."

By now the teaching load was almost too much. Lillian prayed about how to handle the large number of foreign born who wanted to learn English. The answer was simple. The Lord told her, "Take them to the mission and form them into classes."

Many foreign-born students asked about citizenship. "I can read," or "I can speak a little English, but I need help to become an American citizen."

Lillian wrote the Immigration and Naturalization Service in Washington, D.C. She asked them to send her guidelines for preparing a person to become a citizen. Their response was immediate and overwhelming. They sent a trunkful of books and materials to be sorted and sifted. As she worked to condense and prepare the material for study, she prayed for someone to teach a citizenship course.

"Of course," she thought. "Who else could be as caring and conscientious and aware of those principles our country was founded on? Who else loves these people as John does? John is the one!"

Both John and Lillian sensed the beginnings of something exciting when she spoke to him about teaching a citizenship class.

Donald B. Woessner, the new Immigration and Naturalization officer for Fairbanks, was happy to talk with the Isaacs about the proposed citizenship class. He was interested in the people who went through testing in his office. He wanted them well prepared and ready to be good citizens. He listened to the Isaacs' ideas and encouraged them in the venture.

In September 1962 the Isaacs moved the literacy school from their home to the mission and began an English-Citizenship School. Reading on several levels, English as a second language, and citizenship classes were offered. Tutoring was also provided for children.

The foreign born of Fairbanks flocked to the school. When they learned the service was free, they smiled. Soon each one asked, "Why do you do this for us without pay?" This question provided an opportunity to give a witness to God's love.

Teachers from the first workshop came to teach at the school. They volunteered because they loved Jesus, their country, and these people. Other teachers were recruited as needed. At least one workshop was held each year. Many churches were represented in the faculty because the school was a missions project of the state and associational WMU. Their prayer support was also essential.

Christmas was always a special time at the mission. This year, as usual, there would be a program of stories, song, and drama.

Minnie, an Athabascan Indian, came irregularly, but she wanted to sing in the Christmas program. She had a plaintive voice that touched the hearts of the people. She often sang familiar sounding songs which could not be found in any hymnal.

"How did you learn to sing all those songs, Minnie?" John asked one day.

"Why, the angels taught me, Preacher," Minnie answered with a grin.

"What do you mean?" Lillian asked.

"It's a long story. Are you sure you want to hear?"

"Of course we do!" John and Lillian both answered at once.

"When I was six years old, all of us children were playing around the camp one day. Somehow I got a terrible lick on my head that knocked me unconscious. When I came to, I couldn't see anything. My folks just let me rest a day or so thinking I would get better, but I never have seen anything since that day.

"Now, my family were all trappers. When they'd go out to check the traps or to hunt, I would try to follow them by the sound of their voices. But I would stumble and fall over things—rocks or bushes or logs—and I couldn't keep up. Then they would be gone. I couldn't hear their voices any more. I'd call and call, but they couldn't hear me. I was so lonely and afraid that I would cry and cry. Finally, I would find a tree I could climb. I'd go up in the tree and sit there all day. At least I was off the ground and safe from any animals that might come my way. I would sit there all day—sometimes more than a day—until I heard their voices telling me they were coming back."

"You must have been hungry lots of times," John said.

"And worried about falling out of the tree," Lillian added. "Couldn't somebody stay with you or carry you on their shoulders?"

Minnie gave a little chuckle at that thought and went on with her story. "Everybody had a job to do, even the children. They didn't have time to fool with a little blind girl. And really I wasn't worth the bother. I wasn't fit to work any more." Minnie sounded sad as she remembered. "I was afraid of falling out of the tree, of strange sounds, of everything. I cried a lot until one day I heard the most beautiful sound I'd every heard. 'Why, that sounds like angels singing,' I thought. And that's what it was! I was never lonely or sad after that. I knew I could climb my tree and hear that wonderful music. They taught me all of their songs and how to sing them."

"Did you sing for your folks?" John wanted to know. "What did they think?"

"Well, my mother would ask me about certain tunes," Minnie mused as she tried to remember just what they did say. "She said they reminded her of something she heard in a church one time."

Often Minnie would hum a tune and ask someone to look for it in the hymnbook. Sometimes they could find it; sometimes it was not there.

"Minnie," Lillian said thoughtfully, "I think it would be most appropriate for you to sing in the Christmas program. After all, the angels may have taught you some of the very same songs they sang when Jesus was born. That's what we'll be celebrating at Christmas!"

Minnie was thrilled about the program. She was also fascinated by the thoughts of the English-Citizenship School at the mission. "Can I come?" she wanted to know.

"Of course," Lillian assured her.

One night just after Christmas Minnie did come to school.

Lillian and the faculty were faced with a problem. "But how can we teach her? She is blind!" The question was a prayer, and God gave Lillian an answer.

With confidence in the Lord, Lillian turned to the blind girl, "Minnie, what do you want to learn?"

"I want to learn to read. I want to read the Bible."

"Have you ever heard of Braille writing?"

"Yes, I have," answered Minnie. "Somebody taught me the alphabet once, but it's been so long ago that I have forgotten it."

"I have a copy of that alphabet for you," Lillian said. Someone had sent her a copy in the mail just the week before. Not even thinking of Minnie at the time, she had stuck it in her Bible for safe-keeping. Now she simply took it out. Lillian began to thank God for providing the Braille material. "Lord, thank You for taking care of Minnie's needs and mine—even before we are aware we have them. You are so good to us! We love You and will give You the honor as You show us how to teach Minnie to read. Amen."

In a few days Minnie remembered what her fingers had once learned. The First Baptist Church of Fairbanks gave a Braille Bible to Minnie. She ran her fingers over the many volumes. "What book do you want to read first, Minnie?" Lillian asked as they admired them.

"The book of John," Minnie answered strong and clear.

A rather simple solution was reached. Someone would read the book of John from a regular Bible as Minnie followed the Braille letters. In a few weeks she remembered enough to read whole words. Teaching Minnie was a joy and blessing to the privileged reader.

Mary Jane and Jim Netherton were transferred to Alaska. Jim began work on the North Slopes for his oil company. He stayed in Fairbanks one week, then went to the North Slopes for a week. Mary Jane became partially paralyzed on one side of her body after a brain tumor was removed. She was unable to get away from home alone. While Jim was home they shopped for groceries, handled household business, and attended the mission.

One day after praying for Mary Jane, Lillian said, "Mary Jane, we need you to work here at the mission. There are so many jobs you can do."

"I can't do anything," Mary Jane mumbled. "Why I can't go anywhere the weeks Jim is gone."

"John Isaacs will pick you up on the bus. He knows exactly where you live," Lillian offered.

"But I can't walk by myself, much less get on the bus," argued Mary Jane.

"Mary Jane, John can get you on the bus. Blind Minnie can't see a thing, and he gets her on. You can see, so you don't have to worry. He'll be there. Be ready." Lillian refused to take no for an answer.

Mary Jane began to come to the mission to help with English classes and other courses. Lillian always had important work for her to do. Mary Jane faithfully attended Thursday Bible study and Sunday worship services. A six-year-old boy at the mission helped her find something to laugh about. It was the first time she had laughed since her surgery.

The Isaacs inspired Mary Jane to use her free time to pray rather than to think of her own sad plight. "Mary Jane, I want you to pray every day for Ok Cha Taylor, the beautiful girl from Vietnam who comes to the English classes. She needs to believe in Jesus, but she holds on to Buddha. I think the Holy Spirit is speaking to her, so please add her name to your list. Don't skip a single day praying for her. She is special!"

Mary Jane prayed for Ok Cha and unknowingly continued her own therapy as she ministered to others.

Lillian prayed for Ok Cha too. One morning just after this prayertime, Ok Cha appeared at the door. "Come in, come in, and welcome," smiled Lillian. "Why are you out so early in this 55 degrees-below-zero weather?"

"Oh, I come so you help me find a job today," Ok Cha answered as she took off her hat and mittens.

"Sit here a minute," Lillian directed her to the kitchen table. "I'll be right with you." Lillian walked toward her bedroom to think of how to tell Ok Cha the weather was too cold for them to go job hunting. As she walked, she seemed to hear, "Didn't you just pray for Ok Cha?"

"Yes, Lord."

"She needs a job."

"It's too cold. Managers don't hire when it's 55 below."

"You prayed. She's here. She needs a job. Help her."

Lillian put on her parka and boots. They drove all over town and stopped many places.

Lillian was right. Every business manager said, "It's too cold. We don't have any customers, so we don't need more waitresses or dishwashers or saleswomen." As they turned toward home late in the afternoon, Lillian prayed, "Lord, I don't understand. We've looked all day, but we've found nothing."

An almost audible voice answered, "Stop at the dry cleaners at the next corner."

As the car pulled closer, Lillian told Ok Cha, "Stop here."

As they walked in, Lillian greeted her friend, the owner of the cleaners. "I have brought you a good worker," she said.

A few minutes later he gave Ok Cha a job and told her to report Monday at 10:00 A.M.

Ok Cha and Lillian were thrilled. Lillian and the new employer agreed that Ok Cha would not work on Sundays. She could continue coming to the mission for worship and English study.

Lillian and Mary Jane continued to pray for Ok Cha's salvation. One Sunday Ok Cha told Lillian her car was in the shop, and she needed a ride to work the next day.

Lillian knew John would be happy to provide that ride. The only problem was that John was awakened early in the morning to minister to another person. He left immediately and was many miles away before Lillian realized she had never mentioned Ok Cha's need.

Lillian was not worried. She would call someone else to take Ok Cha to work. She called first one then another. No one was available. One person had a sick child she could not leave. Another was away on business. At 9:05 Lillian became discouraged and almost desperate.

Suddenly she felt rebuked. "Lord, I have asked everyone but You. I am ashamed. Will You help me get Ok Cha to work?"

She started to the phone again, trying to decide who to call. But the phone rang before she reached it. When she lifted the receiver, she heard, "Lillian, this is Jim Netherton. Do you need me?"

"Yes," Lillian almost shouted into the phone. "Get here as quick as you can!"

When Jim drove up, Lillian was standing at the side of the street. "No time to tell you where to go. Just drive and I'll tell you when to turn." Lillian directed as she hopped into the car. Between turns,

Lillian asked, "How did you know I needed you?"

"Strange thing!" mused Jim. "Mary Jane was sitting at her desk praying for a list of people. She put her finger on Ok Cha Taylor's name to pray for her just as I walked into the room. She looked up and with unbelievable conviction said, 'Jim, quick call Lillian. She needs you.' You know the rest."

Ok Cha was standing in the ankle-deep snow waiting for her ride. Explanations and discussion followed. Jim joined in to tell his part of the story.

They pulled up to the curb in front of the cleaners at two minutes before ten. As she jumped from the car, Ok Cha pled, "Come in with me! Please!"

She burst through the door. Jim and Lillian heard her exclaim with joy, "Jesus brought me to work!" She repeated it several times to her astounded boss. When he turned to Lillian for an explanation, Ok Cha gathered the other workers to tell them the story. She invited them to look out the store window at the cross on the top of the mission steeple.

"My church," she said proudly, "where I go to pray to Jesus who brought me to work!"

The next Sunday Ok Cha made a profession of faith in "the Jesus who works to answer my prayers. Buddha sits and does nothing. He does not even hear me pray."

As Mary Jane continued to pray for Ok Cha and others, her faith in intercessory prayer was increased. She gained new physical strength and could talk easier. She began to teach a Sunday School class. Eventually, she walked with only a slight limp, and her once drawn face relaxed to a slightly crooked smile.

Jesus had freed both Ok Cha and Mary Jane.

10

Both Sides of the Desk

LILLIAN and John seemed to attract the finest teachers for their faculty. They prayed for each one, and God answered their prayers by sending only the best. Ethel Peasgood is an example.

Ethel turned her life over to the Lord. He moved her from Canada to Alaska. He took care of her as she taught in public schools in Alaska for more than 36 years. She could mush five dogs, navigate on snowshoes, pan for gold, shoot birds, or hunt bears. For part of the 36 years, she was the only teacher in a remote village school. One year she was voted teacher of the year for Alaska. She loved her students, and that love was returned. They cried when they *had* to observe holidays and vacation time.

The Lord led Ethel to the school as it began. The Isaacs depended on her faithfulness and quality teaching.

Rubye Thomas was another early teacher. She served as associational WMU director and learned about the mission. The Isaacs sparked her interest in teaching. She was already a woman of prayer, but her association with Lillian and John made her faith grow. She took Lillian as her role model and often said, "When things don't go right and I want to get ruffled, I say, 'I must be like Lillian Isaacs.' "

Ivy Caudill Brooks, a public health nurse from Kentucky, had been in the literacy workshop in Pineville at Clear Creek Baptist School. She had taught one or two students as she worked at her nursing job in Kentucky. When she transferred from Unalaklett (Alaska) to Fairbanks, she contacted the Isaacs immediately. They put her to work both as a teacher and as a nurse. Eventually, she moved into a room in the basement of the mission.

Because she was a nurse, Ivy worked with many who could not have been reached otherwise. One such person was a pregnant Japanese mother with two sons. She brought her two little boys to the mission while she attended Bible study or worship services. Those two boys were more lively than most. Ivy and others were kept busy taking care of them.

Mrs. Crawford, the regular nursery worker, came to Lillian almost in tears after their first day. "We bowed our heads for the blessing before refreshments," she said, "and when I looked up, those boys had eaten every one of the cookies."

One day the Japanese boys showed up alone. They reported that their mother just lay on the floor and moaned and would say nothing. Ivy was alert and went at once to check. She rushed the young mother to a hospital where her baby was born prematurely. John and Lillian visited her immediately and tried to comfort her when the baby died. Although she was not a Christian, she wanted her baby to have a Christian service. John granted her wish, then came back to the hospital. She wanted every word he had said to be repeated to her—even the prayers.

"Your baby is in heaven. Wouldn't you like to see her again?" John asked.

"Almost you persuade me that your God is," she said sadly. Soon she moved away, and neither the

Isaacs nor Ivy ever knew if she came to believe.

Another teacher was Margaret Wolfe, whose husband taught at the University of Alaska in Fairbanks. Lillian called her and said simply, "Margaret, we need you." Margaret came. Her family also became involved in the mission. One daughter worked in the nursery and another taught English. Her son played the piano.

One of Margaret's students was a lovely Vietnamese girl named Tu. Tu had married an American soldier and had come home with him to Alaska. At first Tu would not hold up her head nor take her hand from her face as she spoke. Lillian discovered Tu had lost two front teeth as a teenager. After a dentist did the necessary repair, Tu smiled and spoke plainly. She had a good mind and learned quickly, but she was slow to believe in Jesus Christ.

One day when she came to see Lillian, she brought a big basket of strawberries. She was distressed about losing an expensive ring her husband had given her. Since she had been berry picking, she thought she lost the ring in the field. Even though she looked, she could not find the ring. She did not want to tell her husband and asked Lillian what to do.

For several weeks, Tu had been under conviction of sin and Lillian knew the Holy Spirit was working with her. "Why don't you ask Jesus to help you?" she asked.

"He do that?" Tu wanted to know. "I not believe in Him."

"He *can* do that, I know."

"I not know. I look some more!" Tu replied.

She did look more. She looked everywhere. Finally in desperation she said, "Jesus, I look everywhere. Mrs. Isaacs say You know where ring is— You know everything—You true God. If that so, tell me where to look."

In a short time Tu was back at the Isaacs' door.

This time she was excited. "Jesus find my ring. Jesus find my ring!" she said over and over. "He tell me in my head where to look. He find my ring."

Eventually, Tu did believe in Jesus. She wanted to be baptized in the mission but the mission had no baptistry. John explained that even though she would be baptized in another church building, she would still be a member of the mission. Tu could not comprehend. John explained again and again.

"No," Tu finally said. "I be baptized here! In mission! No baptistry? Make one! I give money, husband help build. I wait!"

John had believed long before Tu did that the mission needed a baptistry. In fact, he had already drawn the plans and was just waiting for the proper occasion to present the matter. Now seemed to be the right time. Others agreed, and the baptistry was started. Tu's husband, though a faithful member of another church, helped with the construction. Tu was the first person baptized in the new baptistry.

Tu also attended citizenship classes at the mission. When she became a citizen she chose a new name for herself, as many other new citizens do. She chose the name *Cindy* and the initial *I.* Later she confided to a friend, "You know I name for Reverend and Mrs. Isaacs. My name Cindy I. Doty. *I* stand for *Isaacs.*"

Because so many internationals were coming to the Native Baptist Mission, Dr. Cash and the Isaacs felt the mission needed a new name. They selected Friendship Baptist Mission, a name which spoke to the original members as well as the internationals who came there to study and worship.

Augusta Brown was one of the first internationals to come to the school to study English and citizenship. She was found by Liz Hall. One morning Liz came to the Isaacs' home excited and eager for Lillian to go visiting with her. "I have just found a most unusual person. You must come with me now," she said all in one breath as Lillian opened the door.

"Come in a minute for prayer before we go. Have some coffee and tell me about this person," encouraged Lillian.

"She's German," began Liz. "She has several little children and lives at Fort Wainwright." She stopped for a quick sip of coffee. "I asked her if she went to church, or if her children did. She said, 'No,' but when I asked if she wanted to be a Christian, she said, 'Yes.' I knew what to say, but somehow I couldn't find the right words. I knew you could tell her. So, I came to get you. Let's go!"

Lillian immediately went with Liz to visit Augusta Brown. Augusta was eager to learn but needed guidance before she understood baptism. Lillian invited her to church and told her the pastor would visit her. Later Augusta made a profession of faith during a revival. By the time she got her citizenship she even looked like a different person. She told Lillian, "When you came I was ready to kill myself. I had no hope and was tired of living. But hope in Jesus Christ changes everything. I will serve Him." Then she added, "Plenty of people just like me sitting in houses behind four walls waiting for someone to say, 'Come to Jesus. He loves you too.'"

One Tuesday night, Lillian went over to the mission early to get everything ready for the school. In a moment of quiet, she heard soft footsteps upstairs in the sanctuary. Then she heard doors opening and shutting. She went upstairs immediately to see who was there. When she turned on more lights she found Sachi, one of the Japanese women who had come to study English.

"Where He hide?" Sachi asked as she looked under the pews. "Where He is? I look everywhere. Where He hide?"

"Who are you trying to find, Sachi?"

"Where your God? I tell Him thank you for school—English classes."

"Oh," Lillian answered, "Jesus is our God. We have classes for you because we love Him."

Sachi continued looking around as she added. "I want to see Jesus, but I believe in Buddha."

Looking at her watch, Lillian said, "Come, let's go to class. Jesus wants you to be happy. We're so glad you've come to school."

Sachi was happy to be in school. She had come to Fairbanks with her husband, a soldier, and their 13-month-old twins. She knew no one and was lonely in the long hours while her husband was away. Her first night at class she gave Lillian her address.

The next day John and Lillian got ready to go visiting. They prayed for those whom they would visit. They prayed that God would use them to be a blessing and give glory to His name. Sachi was on the list.

They had a hard time finding her trailer, and then no one was at home. They left a picture postcard of the mission and a greeting for her. The next day they returned. Sachi greeted them warmly. "You first visitor I have in Fairbanks—oh, except Avon lady. At first I not buy, but when she come again I buy so she come back. I have somebody talk to me. But why you come?"

"We love Jesus and Jesus loves you," was the Isaacs' reply.

"I believe in Buddha, and I do not know Jesus. But I like your school."

John reassured her. "You are welcome to come to school. You don't have to come to our church, but we would welcome you there too."

"God is good to me—gave me husband, brought me to America, gave me two fine children."

The Isaacs agreed with Sachi on that point. They drank tea and prayed for her relatives who were still in Japan. They played with the children. Lillian invited her to bring her whole family to church. "We have a nursery for your children."

Sachi, like many others, began to come to the Thursday Bible study and to the worship services. John and Lillian visited her many times. One day she said, "I believe in Buddha, but when you say, 'Jesus,' something happens here." She placed her hand over her heart. "When I say, 'Buddha,' nothing happens. Why?"

Lillian prayed as John answered Sachi's question, "Sachi, Jesus is alive. He is God's Son. The Bible is God's Word." He read, " 'For God so loved the world, that he gave his only begotten Son' (John 3:16). Jesus died for your sins. God wants you to believe in Jesus and let Him live in your heart."

Sachi listened intently. John and Lillian knew the Holy Spirit was working with her. When she came to class the next Tuesday, she followed Lillian around everywhere she went—to the office, to the nursery, to the kitchen. Finally, Lillian said, "Go to class, Sachi."

"Write down what happens at the mission every day," Sachi requested.

Lillian wrote and gave the paper to Sachi. But Sachi was not satisfied. "Write it again," she said.

Lillian wrote the daily schedule again and gave it to her. This time, Sachi bowed and said politely, "Thank you. I pin one paper on my window curtian. I know when I look at it what is at the mission. I will save the other. One day God send a friend to my house. I give it to friend to come to the mission too."

John and Lillian continued to pray for Sachi, and after many weeks, she accepted Jesus. "I believe Jesus is the Son of God. I no longer believe in Buddha." She shed many tears then and after her baptism. Every time Sachi came to church she wept. Finally Lillian asked her, "Is there something wrong, Sachi?"

"No," came the reply. "The tears God gives to

me. I wonder why I was in America seven years before somebody told me about Jesus. Why don't more people go to church? Why don't more missionaries go to tell people about Jesus? When I think of these questions, I cry."

Sachi had asked for a Bible. Now she asked for another. The next day while her twins took a nap, she took the Bible and went next door. "My name is Sachi. I live next door. I bring you a Bible book, for you must not have one. If you had one, it would tell you about Jesus. Then you would come to my door and tell me about Jesus." The neighbor was surprised, but she listened as Sachi continued, "My pastor, John Isaacs, will be here soon to tell you more about Jesus. We want to invite you to church. I go now. My babies wake soon. I come back later. I keep praying for you."

Sachi knocked on many doors and gave away many Bibles. Her testimony and methods were simple, but God directed her and used her to win several people to Jesus. One of these was a Jehovah's Witness. When the lady answered Sachi's knock, she said, "I'm a Jehovah's Witness."

Sachi replied, "I'm a Jesus Witness."

"What is a Jesus Witness? What do you believe?" the startled neighbor asked.

Sachi gave her simple testimony. The Holy Spirit spoke to the lady and she gave her heart to Jesus.

Chin Sun was a beautiful young Korean woman. The Isaacs taught her English and citizenship in one of their first classes. She told John and Lillian much about her early life in Korea. Since Chin Sun was the oldest child in her family, she helped care for the other children. She usually carried a sleeping baby on her back as she slipped around the corner to the small Christian church in her town in Korea. There she heard about Jesus for the first time.

Her Buddhist parents punished her for going to church, but she was drawn by the stories of Jesus.

One day at Christmas she was asked to play the part of Mary in the church Christmas play. Her parents objected. But Chin Sun, who usually received many presents from her well-to-do parents, asked for only one present. She wanted to be in the play and have beautiful pieces of fabric to make costumes for the cast. Finally, because she was a favorite of her father, he gave in to her wish.

Chin Sun had believed the Bible was true even before she moved to Alaska. Soon after moving she began going to Friendship Baptist Mission. She accepted Jesus as her Saviour and was baptized.

One particular morning Chin Sun needed a friend. Lillian brought her in out of the cold. "Jesus loves you, Chin Sun. Come in and eat some breakfast." She poured hot tea, made toast, and scrambled eggs. Then she encouraged Chin Sun to eat and relax. Over and over she said, "Jesus loves you, and I love you."

In the next few weeks Chin Sun repeated her breakfast visit. She shared her needs and problems and listened to Lillian pray for her to make good decisions.

One day Chin Sun said, "Mother Isaacs, this is the most desperate time of my life. So many decisions to make! Pray for me every day."

"I do, Chin Sun, and Mr. Isaacs does too," Lillian assured her. She placed her arms about Chin Sun's slender shoulders. "We love you, and Jesus loves you too."

Finally, the hard decision was made. Chin Sun gave up her business, a sauna, and married Steve. They would live in Anchorage. But before they left Fairbanks, he too made a profession of faith in Jesus Christ.

Aunt Elsie loved to read the hymns from the English hymnbook, even though she sang them in Eskimo. When she read the hymn, "Will There Be Any Stars," she said, "That mean I have to win somebody for Jesus." She became excited. "I know who gonna be my star. I gonna tell Minnie. I gonna go her house every day. I gonna sing to her, and I gonna read Bible and pray. Holy Spirit gonna speak to her heart."

Aunt Elsie's prayers, singing, and reading had an influence on Minnie. So did a broadcast worship service. She became interested in the Bible. Minnie, an Eskimo woman over 100 years of age, decided she wanted to come to the mission so she could see the preacher's mouth when he talked.

Aunt Elsie said, "I tell John Isaacs. John Isaacs drive right up to your house. I gonna be here to help shove you on bus!"

Minnie Tucker, fondly known as "Grandma Tucker," went faithfully to the mission for a long time before she made a profession of faith. Many people prayed for her. Lillian often asked how she felt, but never could understand what Grandma said. She prayed to understand what Grandma mumbled. The Lord directed, "Listen to her."

Lillian tried again. "How are you, Grandma?" Again Lillian could not understand the mumbled words, but she persisted. "What's wrong, Grandma?"

"I never happy," Grandma said plainly.

"Why, what's the matter?" But Grandma just sighed.

One day after the service, she told Lillian, "He was here again today, but I didn't go."

"Who are you talking about?" Lillian asked gently.

"The One who talks in my heart. The One who don't walk around on feet—Jesus."

"What did Jesus say?" encouraged Lillian.

"He say Bible is true. Believe it. He talks loud in my heart. He talk so loud I look on either side to see if them fellers hear him talking to me. He say, 'Go to front of church and tell everybody you believe.' " Her voice caught, but she continued, "I

107

too old. I cry tears and wet my pillow many nights. I tell Jesus, 'I will do what you say next Sunday.' But I never do. I sad all the time."

Lillian stretched her arm around this beautiful old Eskimo. "Grandma, we are never too old to do what Jesus tells us to do. Follow Jesus. He will make you happy."

Aunt Elsie was listening too. "Minnie, when Holy Spirit talk to you, you tell Elsie. We go together."

A few weeks later, right in the middle of John's sermon, both women got up, and talking in Eskimo, made their way to the front of the church. John had learned not to be surprised, or upset. "And why do you come?" he asked just as though he had given an invitation.

Grandma looked at Elsie who explained simply, "I bring my friend to Jesus." Then, almost as though speaking in the same sentence she said, "I gonna testimony." She told what the Lord meant to her, how He had saved her, and how He kept her and answered her prayers. Turning to her friend she said, "Now you testimony."

"Do what?" asked the surprised Grandma Tucker.

"Open your mouth and tell what the Lord has done for you."

"Oh," Grandma exclaimed. "I abide in Him, find Him in my heart. For first time in my life I not afraid." She continued to tell how all of her own tribe had died. She joined another tribe only to see them become sick and die also. She moved on to another village. She felt there must be a god somewhere who loved her. She wanted to know this god.

John had preached from Matthew 10:32-33 that day. "Whosoever therefore shall confess me before men, him will I confess before my Father which is in heaven. But whosoever shall deny me before men, him will I also deny before my Father which is in heaven." Grandma concluded, "I recognize Him down here. Now He will recognize me up there."

Later she said Jesus made her a well person. She had been bent over and tottery as she walked. Now she stood erect and walked with sure feet. "My feet not round on bottom anymore,"she explained.

Grandma Tucker knew God was taking care of her. One night after church she came close to freezing to death. A soldier volunteered to take Grandma Tucker home since John had to go in another direction. Unlike John, the young man did not go to the door with her, but put her out and drove away. As she walked toward her door, she dropped her key in the high snowbank beside the path.

"What I gonna do?" she cried out. "Nobody know I outside. Too far, too cold, too dark to walk to some house. I all alone—can't see key in snow. What I gonna do?"

Suddenly, she stopped short. " 'Scuse me, Lord," she said. "You here with me. You know everything. You know where key drop. Send Holy Spirit to help me find key so I not freeze to death. I gonna get stick by door and whack in snow. You tell me where to whack. *Quiana, Agaune.* Jesus gonna help me."

As Grandma told the story to the Isaacs later, she added, "Holy Spirit smart. He find key on first whack. I sleep warm in my house. *Quiana, Agaune* (Thank You, God)."

Grandma Tucker often talked of light. When John stood to preach, she would say, "I see light brighter than sunlight stand by him when he read God's book, and when he tells people to come to Jesus. When they come I see light bigger." Aunt Elsie agreed, for she saw the same light.

John and Lillian were concerned that Grandma Tucker learn to read the Bible for herself. They asked her many times to come to class. After the worship service one day, Lillian spoke of it to her again. "I was hoping you'd ask me one more time. I want to learn Jesus' name. I go home with you today. After lunch, you show me how to read."

Lillian had been at the mission since 8:00 that day. Much of that time she had been teaching. After lunch she was ready for a nap, or at least a little resting time. She asked Grandma to rest with her.

"You show me to read now," Grandma insisted. "Naps is just for old folks and babies."

Grandma really needed glasses to read, but it was Sunday and businesses were closed. So, Lillian got a felt-tip marker to make large letters for her. Even with the large letters Grandma seemed unable to understand. Suddenly she stopped trying. "Is this the 'portant name?"

"The 'portant name?" Lillian asked.

"There is only one 'portant name and that is Jesus and don't you forget it! You know my name's not 'portant and your name's not 'portant—only Jesus," said Grandma.

When Lillian nodded, she continued, "We started wrong. We gonna start over. We pray first. I gonna pray in Eskimo. God understands it better."

While Grandma prayed in Eskimo, Lillian prayed in English. God answered both of them immediately. After they said, "Amen," Lillian took Grandma's hand and traced the letters J E S U S, the 'portant name.

"Do that again," directed Grandma.

Again, Lillian traced the letters, saying each one as she made it in the wrinkled, brown hand. Then she thanked God for the understanding that she saw brighten Grandma's face.

"I can write Jesus!" Grandma said as she took the marker and began to practice the letters Lillian had traced in her hand. "I know Jesus and I know His name! Thank You, God, thank You! And thank You for my pencil," she said as she dropped the

110

marker into the pocket of her *kuspuc* (dress).

"You can come to my house Friday and we study again. You bring lunch—for everybody there," said Grandma.

"Oh," Lillian asked, "how many will be there?"

"How I know? Today Sunday. How I know who come on Friday? Holy Spirit tell you. You know then. I pray for you."

Grandma and several of her friends did gather to study on Friday. When the Isaacs arrived they saw that Grandma had written the name of Jesus on the calendar, on the grocery bag, on the cracker box. Everywhere there was a little space she had written the 'portant name—Jesus—the name of the one she loved.

John and Lillian made regular Friday visits to Grandma. Her mind was quick, and in a short time she learned many words. She prayed that God would strengthen her eyes. Her prayers were answered. Her sight did improve and she was able to read her Bible every day.

Johnny, summer missionaries, and Christian students from the English-Citizenship School went with the Isaacs to visit Grandma. Chin Sun Stevenson went often. She loved all of the older Eskimo women. "Eskimos and Koreans both Mongolian—very close kin," she would say as she placed her arms around Aunt Elsie and Grandma Tucker.

The Isaacs went to see Grandma Tucker on other days also. She always greeted them cheerily as though she knew they were coming. One day Lillian asked her about that fact. "Oh, I know when you come." With a little encouragement, she told Lillian about her oatmeal box.

"Every morning I get up, go to door to look see if I see Jesus coming. You know, He coming back. Then I go get oatmeal box from cupboad. Just enough for me to eat. I cook, say 'Quiana Agaune,' eat, put box back in cupboad. Next day, the same.

111

Always enough oatmeal in box. Then someday no oatmeal in box. I say, 'Quiana, Agaune, I know You send food today.' You and Brother Isaacs or someone always come."

Missionary J. D. Back (left) talks with Grandma Tucker (center) and John Isaacs (right) (1972).

Aunt Elsie, 79-year-old member of Friendship Baptist Mission, standing in front of her home (1967).

11
Change of Pace

EVERY two years the Isaacs went outside, to the "Lower Forty-Eight," for a period of two months. This was according to the Home Mission Board policy. As the time came close, the Isaacs would pray for God to send just the right persons to take care of their responsibilities at the mission. Once the answer came in the persons of Sam and Betty Gilson.

Sam was in the military when the Isaacs first met him and his wife, Betty. Although they were members of another church, they liked to visit the mission because they found opportunity for service there. They gave money regularly to the mission.

Early in Sam's military career, Betty was led to pledge $20 for the Annie Armstrong Easter Offering. She did not have the money, but asked the Lord to provide it. When the day for giving came, the money was not in hand, so Betty put an IOU in the collection plate. A few days later Sam got a promotion and a $20 raise. Other promotions followed. Because of Betty, every raise was given to God.

One Sunday when John gave the invitation, Sam

114

went forward. He told John he had never had a personal experience with Jesus. He had joined the church as a youngster just because the other guys were doing it. He wanted to make a genuine commitment of his life to Jesus Christ.

The Gilsons became involved in doing volunteer missions work after Sam left the military. John and Lillian felt comfortable leaving the mission in the Gilsons' dedicated hands.

Visits outside were to be times of refreshment and rest, but John and Lillian stayed busy the entire time. Usually John held one or two revival meetings. The Mission Center in Bristol, Virginia, was always on the schedule. Sam and Grace Faulkenberry were working there. People flocked to the center to hear the Bible taught or preached and to listen to stories from Alaska.

One revival at Bristol was especially meaningful. Nearly everyone had left the center after the evening service. A car drove up and a young man and woman got out. They hurried into the center.

"Don't leave. Don't leave yet!" the young man begged. The couple walked rapidly toward the few persons who were still gathered around the Isaacs. The talking ceased, and all eyes turned toward the couple. "Aren't you Reverend Isaacs?" the young man inquired.

"Yes I am," John replied. "How can I help you?"

"I want to become a Christian," he answered. "My name is Buddy Phipps. My father was Adolphe Phipps, 'The Little Chief.' We lived in Neon, Kentucky. I was just a little feller when I came with my father and mother to Pineville to see y'all. But I remember, and I figure that any person who could tell my father how to be saved could help me find Jesus too." John and Buddy shook hands warmly. Then Buddy turned to Lillian and extended his hand. Instead of taking that hand, Lillian put her arms around him and told him how much they loved his family.

"And now you want to become a Christian?" John asked, getting to the purpose of the visit with obvious pleasure.

"Yes, sir."

The small group sat nearby to pray while John talked with young Phipps and his wife. Buddy accepted Jesus as Saviour.

"You know," he said, after a few minutes, "I was reading the paper last night when I saw that you and Mrs. Isaacs were here. I saw tonight was the last night of the revival. Something spoke to my heart. I just had to get here! I knew you could help me. So when I got off work today, I went to get my wife, and we drove here as fast as we could. I'm so thankful we were not too late!"

The times outside meant visits to see family members in North Carolina and Tennessee and Florida. And it meant speaking engagements for the Home Mission Board.

Because they were so busy outside, the Isaacs needed to rest occasionally while they were still on the field. Taking a real break was almost impossible. Lillian actively looked for a way to find time and quiet to make reports, write articles, read, and get spiritual refreshment as well as physical rest. The Lord, as though He were smiling at the time problem, gave her an idea that worked over and over.

"Be quiet in the middle of somebody else's hustle and hurry," the instructions said. "Go to the airport. Nobody will bother you there."

John started taking Lillian to the busy Fairbanks airport periodically. With briefcase in hand, she picked her place away from the crowd and sat down to take her mini vacation. She felt set apart from everybody else's busyness, and knew she was free from interruptions. After a restful morning and a good lunch, she was ready for John to pick her up.

John handled stress differently. He got away from the pressures of his work by changing scenery and helping somebody else work. He was a popular speaker for retreats and revivals, for summer youth camps, and for pastors conferences. He was in demand as a Bible teacher. Some of his favorite places were in the far north above the Arctic Circle. Several times he worked with Valeria Sherard in the native villages around Kiana. He always came home with stories about the Eskimo children. His stories about RA and GA camp on an island were especially interesting. He told about building a fire in a stove that exploded and about carrying water from a river for a chilly bath. Once he lost his footing and almost slid into the river.

One year John went up to Fort Yukon to be in a revival with Missionary Don Rollins. While he was there Don took him for his first and only experience in mushing with a fast Eskimo dog team. About this experience John would only say, "Those dogsleds don't have any springs in them!"

Every year John planted a garden on the back part of the property on Lacey Street. Gardening became his hobby. He grew vegetables and berries, Alaska style. He often sent a 15-or 20-pound turnip or cabbage home with a visitor. And he kept his own table supplied with fresh produce.

He brought in a big basket of cabbages once. "Sweet," he called to Lillian, "I have a good surprise for you. Look at all of these fine cabbages from the garden. How about making us some sauerkraut?"

Lillian still did not claim to be a kitchen genius but she had learned to set a meal for many people in a short time. She kept a stock of groceries on hand to take care of whoever came to Sunday dinner. She never forgot her first Thanksgiving dinner in Kentucky!

Today she did not have time to reminisce. "Why, John, you are the only one around here who eats sauerkraut. When you want some, I'll get it for you from the store. But I *will* take care of those beautiful cabbages for you." Lillian chuckled to herself as she thought of how many students from the school would soon be eating cabbage.

Many times the Isaacs took short trips to Mount McKinley, the glaciers, and other places of interest. Johnny often went on camping trips with Ivy Brooks and other friends. Only once in the 12 years the Isaacs were in Alaska did they plan a real family vacation.

The Isaacs packed their fishing gear one summer and drove to Valdees to go salmon fishing. Salmon fishing is great sport in Alaska. Mission members often talked of catching small ones—maybe 30 to 40 pounds—which they cooked on the riverbank. They brought the larger ones of 80 pounds home for their rooftop freezers. As they drove, John and Johnny visualized all sorts of wonderful times ahead. Lillian looked forward to catching up with her reading. They thanked God they did not feel the pressure of bringing home a meat supply for the winter as the Eskimos did. This was to be a time of fun!

John and Johnny fished the first day, and had big plans for the second. That morning as they started out, Lillian put down her book and walked toward the river with them. "John, I feel we need to go home today."

"Now, Sweet, we have another whole day after today." He called to Johnny who was racing ahead, "Be there in a minute, Son, don't get too far ahead!"

"I don't know," Lillian admitted, "I just feel we ought to go home today."

"Can you think of any reason? Did we forget a meeting? Let's talk about it later," John said on the run. "I've got to catch up with Johnny. See you at lunchtime."

They were gone. Lillian tried to read, but was restless. Maybe she should go for a walk, she thought. That did not satisfy the feeling they should go home.

Meanwhile, the fishermen were having a terrible time. They broke their hooks and lost their lines. They came in long before lunchtime. Lillian was already packed and insisted they leave, although she still did not know why.

They left soon, and arrived home by late afternoon. The day was a summer scorcher. The heat soaked away energy and they all felt exhausted.

"I'm so tired I'm going on to bed now," John announced.

"Me too," echoed Johnny.

Lillian began to put away the vacation gear. She thought she too would go to bed early. "Here are the lemons I forgot to take," she laughed to herself as she picked up the bag and started toward the refrigerator. She rerouted her steps when the phone rang.

"Hello," she answered sleepily. She looked at her watch and realized they had been home less than 20 minutes.

"Lillian, this is Dennis Wolstenholme, from the Immigration and Naturalization office in Anchorage. I'm here in Fairbanks and need to see you. I have our regional director here from Washington, D.C. We are having a time trying to explain our Alaska operation to him. Can you give us some time? This is urgent."

"Of course, Mr. Wolstenholme. When do you want to come?" Lillian looked around the kitchen and at herself. She hoped he would say late tomorrow.

"We will be there in 15 minutes." This answer jarred Lillian awake. Fifteen minutes! How could she get ready in 15 minutes?

If it were not so hot! If only my head did not ache! Lillian's thoughts raced. She saw the bag of lemons still in her hand, and decided to make a large pitcher of lemonade for the men. As she worked she reviewed facts. Mr. Wolstenholme was the district director of the Immigration and Naturalization Service. The United States was divided into ten districts. Alaska was one of them. He was bringing with him one of the four regional directors.

Lillian finished making the lemonade and cleared the kitchen table. She barely had time to straighten her hair and her skirt before the two men arrived.

Mr. Wolstenholme introduced Lillian to the regional director. Both men spoke of the unusual heat. They sat at the kitchen table while Lillian poured tall glasses of iced lemonade. Before the conversation began she poured refills for her guests.

Mr. Wolstenholme started the questions. "Mrs. Isaacs, will you explain how we prepare people for citizenship here—at your Citizenship School?"

"Well, there are several things you need to know first about our Alaska Immigration and Naturalization officers," Lillian began. Mr. Wolstenholme looked up from his lemonade and cleared his throat. Lillian continued as though she had neither seen nor heard. "We have the finest officers to be found anywhere in the United States. They meet our needs efficiently and cheerfully. They have service as their aim. Their service is for the individual, and in serving the individual they serve the nation, and eventually the world."

Mr. Wolstenholme relaxed. Lillian refilled the lemonade glasses. Then she continued. "You know Alaska is different from all the other districts. We do not have immigrants from only one country, for example, or from one area even. The world has come here to live." She began to explain how the English-Citizenship School got started, how the Washington office had sent the information, and how carefully John taught. She told about the graduation ceremony, the tests—even the New Citizen Cup. She concluded by applauding again the immigration officers who worked so closely with them.

120

"Tell about Grandma Tucker and Aunt Elsie," encouraged Mr. Wolstenholme.

Lillian refilled their lemonade glasses a third time before she told several stories about the older Eskimos. She told also about Ok Cha, Tu, Augusta, and others. At times the men laughed. At times they wept.

Finally, the regional director said, "Mrs. Isaacs, I have just one question. How much do you charge for the service you do for us and for these people?"

Lillian smiled, "Nothing! We do not charge at all. We do it in the name of Jesus."

There was a moment of silence. Then both directors stood. "Wolstenholme, I have found out everything I need to know. Alaska gets only top rating in this investigation. I'm ready to fly to Washington and make my report." He turned to shake Lillian's hand. As he glanced at the empty lemonade pitcher, he added, "Never have I been more refreshed in body and spirit. I'm so happy to have heard about your good school!"

After the two men left, Lillian sat down at the table again. "Thank You, Father, for good men like these two directors who make our work for You easier. Bless them as they travel." Then she added, "And thank You that my headache is gone, and I don't even feel tired. You are so good! Amen."

"Mama, lots of people are already coming into the mission. They're packing sandbags around the walls of the basement. You ought to see all the water in Lacey Street," Johnny reported to Lillian.

"Maybe the rain will stop soon, and the river will go down. The radio announcer just said most people near the Chena have already moved out. I guess Grandma Tucker is safe by now since she left yesterday. Do any of your school friends live over there, Johnny?" Lillian tried to make conversation with Johnny. But Johnny had grabbed what he came for and run back to help those gathering into the mission. Many came to the mission for safety because it was the highest point in the community.

Lillian began to prepare food to send to those at the mission. She thought just a moment or two had gone by. Suddenly both John and Johnny were at the door. Lillian stared at them unbelieving. They were wet up to the waist.

"Get a wrap, Sweet. You have to go now," John directed. The mission basement and ours are both flooded. The water is still rising." He boxed the items Lillian had gathered. She ran for her boots and some warm clothes.

"Hurry, Mama, or we won't make it!" urged Johnny.

John, arms high over his head to keep the provisions dry, led the way. He tried to find a safe path for Johnny and Lillian.

"I can't believe . . . so much water!" Lillian exclaimed as they waded into the flooded street—up to their ankles, their knees, now their waists and beyond!

"Hold my arm, Mama. It's moving so fast, it could knock you down in a minute," instructed Johnny.

"So cold!" Lillian whispered. A chill ran through both of them but they kept moving. They were almost halfway there.

"What's the matter, Mama?" Johnny shouted at Lillian as she hesitated, then stumbled. "You all right?"

Lillian clutched at her chest and whispered, "Got to . . . catch . . . my . . . breath."

Johnny, alarmed, half lifted her, and slipped her arm over his shoulder. Together they struggled toward the spot where the steps should be. His shouts brought help. Ivy Brooks took charge when they entered the sanctuary.

Ivy wrapped Lillian in blankets, put her to bed, and massaged her feet to encourage the circulation. She shouted directions. "Get some more blankets.

122

Bring some hot tea for her. The shock of that ice water out there has almost stopped her heart! Hurry!"

Lillian revived, but was pale and weak. There was little time for her to rest, but Ivy insisted she keep trying. Other refugees kept coming. And the muddy, dark water kept rising.

The next day John and Lillian looked outside at the swirling water. Another three-inch rise would bring it inside the sanctuary. More than 50 people had slept on the pews or in sleeping bags on the floor. The August night chilled them. The seriousness of the situation caused worry and fear.

John and Lillian had spent most of the night in prayer. John decided to take his regular place at the pulpit. He got the attention of the group and announced, "We must pray the water will not rise anymore."

After a season of prayer, he added, "Since we'll be here together for a while we must have some understandings to guide us. Mrs. Isaacs will talk with you about that."

Lillian stood next to the mattress where she had rested. "We have prayed, and through faith we know God can hold the water outside. Inside there will be no complaining. We will sing and pray and have Bible study. When we have food, we will share. We are reasonably warm and dry. We have a nurse and medicine for any who are sick. The bathroom works. We have much to be thankful for."

A few hours later, a shout of praise went up when everyone realized that though the water was level with the doors, it rose no more and never came inside. Personnel from the Health Department came by in a boat, tested the water, and announced it safe for drinking. Amazingly enough the electricity worked. A hot plate, moved from the kitchen earlier, provided heat for coffee. Someone brought in food by boat.

"What do we need most?" John asked a few days later. Someone with a great deal of forethought said, "A boat! We need a boat!"

"Then we will pray for a boat," Lillian announced. During the prayertime that followed, they heard a shout from outside. Lillian went to the door.

"You can stop asking and start thanking," she said as she returned to the group. "Our boat is here."

A friend had seen a rowboat with two oars floating down Cushman Street. He immediately got into his own boat, caught the loose one, and towed it one block to the mission. "I just had a feeling you folks needed this boat," he said. "Can I get anything else for you?"

It was two weeks before the water receded, the refugees could return home, and cleanup could begin. Those days were filled with miracles.

The basement at the mission had flooded in spite of all efforts to keep the water out. An engineer told the Isaacs, "If the water had not come in, the walls would have collapsed from the outside pressure. How you had standing walls, clean water in the pipes, plumbing that worked, and electricity upstairs is the greatest miracle of all. No one else around here did."

John smiled. "Well the Lord just worked to keep us! Guess we'll need another miracle though to get all of the mud and mess out of this basement!"

But the Lord gave muscle power instead. The Southern Baptist Brotherhood Commission sent more than 100 men to Alaska to help repair flood damaged churches. Pan Am flew them free of charge. The Home Mission Board sent money needed for supplies. Eventually the mission was in good repair.

Grandma Tucker's small house was one of many ruined by the water. The owner decided the cost to repair it would be more than its value to him.

Grandma was distressed, and went to God for help. God moved the members of the mission to answer her prayers. They had already worked on the churches and on their own homes. They made all necessary repairs on Grandma's house and put it in better condition than it was before. In return, the owner let Grandma Tucker live there rent free.

John pauses for a rest at Friendship Baptist Mission after the flood (1967).

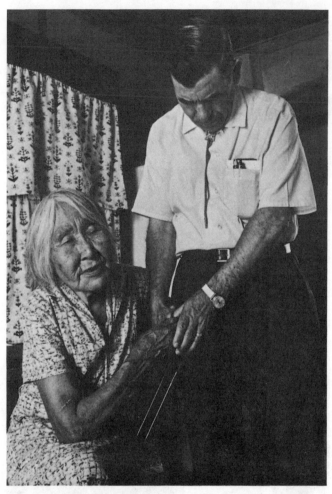

John prays with 107- or 108-year-old Grandma Tucker.

12
Help for Growing

THE Isaacs worked closely with the Immigration and Naturalization Service of Alaska from the beginning of the English-Citizenship School in 1962. Donald Woessner was the officer assigned to Fairbanks. At the completion of each course, students went into Mr. Woessner's office individually for their tests. He was invited to come to the school several times during each term so the students could get to know him. He thanked the Isaacs for this opportunity. He explained, "Those who have never worked with naturalized citizens cannot appreciate the apprehension of these candidates. To them, the Immigration and Naturalization officer has the power of making or crushing their futures. I appreciate all you do to eliminate that fear."

After each group of students passed the test there was a graduation ceremony at Friendship Mission. Graduations were occasions for great joy and celebration. The program featured the students singing in their native language and telling why they wanted to be United States citizens. Others told why they studied English. The associational WMU recognized the teachers, the immigration officer presented certificates, and an outstanding guest gave a graduation address.

After the ceremony all guests were invited to the fellowship hall which had been decorated by the students. The students and their families were arrayed in colorful national dress. The coffee table was always attended by one of Fairbanks most outstanding citizens. This woman used her own silver service, china cups, and lace or linen cloth, which added dignity to the affair. Happy voices and delicious aromas filled the air. The tables held an international smorgasbord, also prepared by the students.

Graduations were popular and well attended. The speakers felt honored to be asked. They were carefully chosen as Lillian prayed about the programs. Sometimes a district or local Immigration and Naturalization officer would be asked. Sometimes the judge of the court, or a Home Mission Board representative, or a national WMU figure would give the address.

Once Lillian heard God directing her to ask General Jones, the ranking officer at Fort Wainwright to be the graduation speaker. He proved to be a good choice. Many of the students were wives of soldiers stationed at his post. The general seemed to sense the importance of his task, and arrived in full dress uniform with all military flair and flurry.

The mission was packed. Speeches were well rehearsed. Festivity and food were ready downstairs. The Isaacs always asked some of the Alaskan people to sing or to read Scripture or to make speeches about English or reading classes. On this occasion, Aunt Elsie was to sing. She sat, dressed in her coloful cotton *kuspuc,* and held her program as long as she could. Finally, she tapped loudly on the program and spoke to Lillian in a loud whisper, "Is it my turn yet?"

Lillian put her off as quietly as possible. Finally her time came. Aunt Elsie went to the platform and sang a hymn in Eskimo. She sang all of the stanzas. When she received a round of applause, she sang another hymn—all stanzas.

Then Aunt Elsie went to the front of the platform and sat with her feet hanging off. John thought she had chosen to sit there for the rest of the program and arose to introduce the next speaker. Aunt Elsie was indignant. "I not finished," she announced. "Sit down."

Then with the flourish of a professional she took a French harp from her pocket and played another hymn. A clapping audience encouraged another, and another.

John looked at Lillian. Lillian looked at John. They both sighed, for it seemed they were to have an impromptu program that evening. Finally, Aunt Elsie got up from her seat on the floor and stood directly in front of General Jones. "I gonna testimony," she announced.

In her broken English, she gave a simple testimony of what Jesus meant to her. Then she began to quote, "For God so loved the world. . . ." She stepped aside and turned to the general. "That mean *you*," she said quietly to him. "You understand?" When the general nodded she turned back to the audience for the next phrase. "That he gave his only begotten son. . . . That Jesus," she said as she turned to the general again. "You understand?" she queried, with quiet dignity. After his nod, she turned to the audience. Phrase by phrase, she finished the verse, turning after each one to ask the general if he understood.

By now, the silence and stillness of the room were electrifying. John was fascinated, and sat staring at what was going on. Lillian was praying that the general would not be offended and would still give his address (if he ever got the chance). She wondered if she should add a petition for the floor to open and let her fall to the basement taking Aunt Elsie with her. But she too felt a sense of awe in the air.

129

When Aunt Elsie finished John 3:16, she went immediately to Romans 3:23. "You a sinner," she said to the general. "You understand?" When the general nodded, this amazing Eskimo woman proceeded through the entire plan of salvation in the same manner she had started. No one stirred as Aunt Elsie prayed at the end of her speech. She sat down in the audience with dignity and confidence. The hush was finally broken by several sniffs, a little nose blowing, and an open sob.

John stood and called for the next part on the program. The general rose, and with grace and poise said he had never been so moved in his life as he was by Aunt Elsie's speech. He thanked her, and then gave his own prepared address.

Immediately after the program, Lillian gave the general a gift, a face painted by Aunt Elsie. She enclosed in the package an explanation of how it came to be. Then she told the general, "The program has been long. I'm sure all of us will understand if your duties make it necessary for you to leave now. Thank you so much for coming."

"No!" General Jones replied. "I've never seen a woman like Mrs. Willock, nor a place like this one in my life. I can hardly wait to get downstairs!" The two went together to the festivities.

The next morning as Lillian was making plans for the day, the phone rang. General Jones' secretary said the general wanted to speak with her. "Of course," Lillian answered and smiled as she thought of all the things the general might say if she were in the military. To her surprise, he thanked her again for asking him to speak at the ceremony.

"God was in that place," he declared. Then he wanted to know more about Aunt Elsie. He was impressed with the face Aunt Elsie had made and wanted to order 10,000 of them for someone to sell. "Then you'll have all the money you need for your work," he said.

Lillian laughed as she explained some of the complications of such a project. She thanked him for his idea, but declined to use it.

Then the general wanted to know more about the school and the mission. Lillian gladly gave him more information.

"Mrs. Isaacs," General Jones added after a lengthy conversation, "if I can ever help you and Mr. Isaacs, in any way, let me know. Just call the number I have given you. You can reach me there at any hour. And thank you again for asking me to come last night."

"And thank You, Lord," Lillian prayed as she hung up the phone. "Thank You for putting such a fine man in a high place in our military. Thank You for the help he will be able to give us for Your glory. Amen."

Later in the day, John and Lillian went to visit Aunt Elsie. She was glad to see them. "The general called me this morning," Lillian began. Aunt Elsie ignored the remark. Lillian continued, "He asked about you, Aunt Elsie." She gave no response, except a slight shrug of her shoulders.

"Aunt Elsie, he's the military man who was at the graduation last night."

"Lotsa GIs there. Me not know one from other," said Elsie.

"This is the one you talked to—on the platform— the one with all the medals and ribbons on his uniform."

"Oh, the big soldier," Aunt Elsie shrugged again. "Holy Spirit say give him message. Me do it. When Holy Spirit say you do something, you do it."

The rest of the day went as usual. That conversation was closed as far as Aunt Elsie was concerned.

The graduation and reception at the mission were just parts of becoming a citizen once the applicant passed the test. The official naturalization ceremony took place in the US District Court in downtown Fairbanks. There the applicants and their families came, dressed in their best clothes. The Isaacs had impressed upon them the importance of looking their best. Petitioners from the school at the mission searched the audience until they spotted their teachers. Then they settled down to the business at hand. The Isaacs were always present.

After the court was convened, the presiding judge made his opening remarks. Several judges took turns to sit for this occasion, but Judge Warren Taylor was called upon most often. He showed much interest in the school at the mission and came often to the graduations. The naturalization ceremony included patriotic music followed by a speaker chosen by the court. Then Mr. Woessner, the examiner, presented each petitioner to the court. Each stood as his or her name was called. The solemnity of the ceremony was broken only occasionally by a child's soft cry, or a nervous cough. Emotions ran high.

Congratulations were offered to the new citizens after they received their naturalization papers from the clerk of the court. None was more sincere nor carried so much love as those words from the Isaacs. John usually would say, "You are a new citizen, an important person in this country. Mrs. Isaacs and I would like to invite you to have tea with us in our home."

Each new citizen from the school received this invitation and came alone or with his or her family. Each individual was entertained as royally as the head of state in his or her former country would have been. Lillian arranged for special cake or cookies, and served tea (or coffee) in a china cup marked with gold lettering that announced, "New Citizen of the United States." John offered a prayer of thanksgiving for the new citizen and his or her family, and prayed for any family members still in another country. Each received a beautiful Bible. Further appointments were made to talk about becoming a citizen of God's kingdom if the honoree had not done so already.

Louise Yarbrough, the WMU executive secretary for Alaska, had found the New Citizen Cup in Anchorage. She knew at once where it belonged. On a visit to Fairbanks she presented it to the Isaacs.

Louise had encouraged the state WMU to help sponsor the literacy workshops in Fairbanks and the Citizenship School. Louise had become more and more interested. By 1964 she invited Lillian to hold a workshop in Anchorage. This workshop was the beginning of an English-Citizenship School at Grandview Baptist Church in Anchorage. With Lillian's help, it was patterned after the one in Fairbanks.

By the time this new school was founded, the Immigration and Naturalization Service had transferred Mr. Woessner to Anchorage. He was ready to lend support and encouragement. He said: ". . . Although I am not a Baptist, I really do commend you people for the excellent work you are doing in Anchorage and Fairbanks. We recommend your schools to all who . . . ask about learning to speak English and learning the things necessary to qualify them to become citizens of this country."

Later Lillian went with Louise to several other cities. When Judy Rice followed Louise as WMU executive secretary, Judy continued to encourage literacy all over the state. She invited Lillian, still the best resource person, to conduct workshops in other cities. The work was spreading.

Bible study at the mission continued to grow. All foreign born in the school were invited to come. Many came because the study was in English.

By now a large group met at 10:00 A.M. each Thursday. They stayed at least until 12:00 and many times until 2:00. At first Lillian prepared a light lunch for everyone while John conducted the study. But the increased numbers outgrew her lone efforts. As she prayed about this pleasant problem,

133

she learned that professional help was available to her and the members of the class. She invited the extension service of the University of Alaska at Fairbanks to come and demonstrate a different phase of nutrition each week. The Isaacs had observed the dietary habits of many of the Eskimos as well as the foreign born. Both groups needed nutritional guidance. The extension service showed students how to grow or catch food that was native to this environment, how to prepare it, and how to preserve it at home. The class members learned as they enjoyed the good meals used for the demonstration. And Lillian enjoyed her new freedom from the kitchen.

At other times Lillian and John invited Ivy Brooks or another of the public health personnel to teach hygiene, preventive medicine, or general health. Again the students benefited.

One of the regular members of the study group came up with another idea. "Mr. Isaacs," Ella Maurer said, "we learn other things that help us if we stay after we have our Bible study on Thursday. But we'd like to add to the school at night too. How about a Bible course at the English-Citizenship School?"

The Isaacs considered the request a good one, and Bible courses were added. One of the local pastors taught, varying the content from term to term. This course became one of the most popular at the school.

The curriculum for the English-Cititzenship School was flexible and grew further. As needs were discovered, courses were added. Eventually students came to study English at all levels, citizenship, driver education, spelling, health, math or arithmetic, cooking, and Bible.

All phases of work at the mission expanded. The school and Bible study continued during the summer. Added to that was Vacation Bible School, recreation, and Bible study for children. Various

134

workers came for short periods of time to help. Each time the Isaacs went outside to speak, they drew a new group of volunteers from the "Lower Forty-Eight." Many were WMU members. Others came from the Home Mission Board and other agencies to do specific jobs. For example, the Isaacs invited Mildred Blankenship, director of literacy work for the Board, to help with workshops.

Each summer, the Board sent one or more summer missionaries to work at Friendship Baptist Mission. Their instructions were to "do whatever the Isaacs do, or say needs to be done."

Cathy Belew was one of those summer missionaries. "She could do anything!" Lillian reported. And Cathy thought if Lillian and John said she could do a job, she could do it. She did the usual work such as teaching Vacation Bible School, visiting prospects, planning recreation, and teaching children. She liked best the extras the Isaacs had become known for doing. She visited Grandma Tucker and read to her, helped her with shopping, or cleaned her house.

Cathy attended the English-Citizenship School each week. There she did as Johnny did. That meant she did whatever needed to be done that was not assigned specifically to someone else. At times both taught reading or English, helped in the nursery, made refreshments, kept records, drove students home, or picked them up for class.

Eskimos of all ages loved Cathy and liked to hear her sing and play her guitar. And she enjoyed performing for them. At any time when activities got a little slow, John or Lillian would say, "Now Cathy is going to play and sing for us."

Almost automatically they would form a circle around her as she took her guitar from the case. She sang as though the program had been planned for days, announcing one number after another, and involving old and young alike in her special music.

"I wish we could keep Cathy," John said one morning as the summer was coming to a close. Before Lillian could speak her hearty agreement, Johnny added his word.

"Me too! It sure is nice having another teenager around here."

Lillian wanted to attend the state convention that summer. She never had been able to go because of the school. That year she gave instructions to Cathy and Johnny, and left them in charge. They did their best. When Lillian returned, many said they never knew she was absent.

One of Cathy's favorite assignments was to read to blind Minnie as she followed the words in her Braille Bible. She shared this responsibility with others, though.

Two young soldiers appeared at the school one evening late in the summer. One had visited the mission many times on Sundays. He spoke to Lillian, "Mrs. Isaacs, maybe you can do something with this guy I have out in my car. I picked him up hitchhiking on the way to town. He says he's bored and doesn't have anything to do and doesn't really want to get drunk. I told him everybody is welcome at the mission. Can he do something around here?"

"Of course he can," smiled Lillian. "We always can use another helper."

The young soldier turned to leave. As he closed the door, he stuck his head back inside to add, "Oh, yeah! I better mention—he says he's an atheist."

He was gone before Lillian could ask further questions. Before the hitchhiker came in, she took time to pray, "Lord, there must be something an atheist can do for You. Help me to know just what it is. Thank You for answering quickly. Amen."

The newcomer, a young man named Mike, was reserved at first. He repeated the information Lillian already had learned from his friend. He stressed the fact he was an atheist. Lillian showed him around the school, hinting at some ways he could be of help. Nothing interested him. Finally, he stated firmly, "I know what I want to do! I'm a good teacher, and I want to teach. I liked this place when Joe told me about it because it was a school. I want to teach!"

Lillian was a little surprised, but she spoke as though she weren't. "Well, I'll tell you what you have to do if you teach here. First, you have to come every Tuesday night—rain, sleet, snow, or whatever. And you have to be on time. You also have to be willing to do other jobs you may be asked to do. Can you do that?"

Mike thought a minute. "Yes, I can! I can arrange my work at the post so Tuesday night will be my time off. I can do it."

"Wait here a moment," Lillian instructed. "I'll see if your student is here yet." She prayed silently, "Thank You, Lord, for Your answer."

When she returned a few minutes later, she said, "You start tonight." She directed the soldier toward the small classroom where an Indian girl sat waiting. As the door opened, the student lifted her sightless eyes, and a broad smile crossed her face.

"Hello," she said, extending her hand.

"Mike," Lillian said, "This is Minnie. She's blind, and she's learning to read Braille. This is her book." She handed him the thick volume of the Gospel of John. "Your job is to read from this book as she follows the Braille letters," she continued as she gave him a regular English New Testament. "You must read slowly and clearly and repeat as many times as she asks you so she can learn as she goes. Any questions?" Then she opened the Braille book for Minnie and the New Testament for Mike.

Mike gulped. "Uh, no ma'am," he answered. He pushed the heavy volume nearer Minnie and pulled up a chair for himself.

Lillian closed the door and left. She had alerted

Minnie that her reader for the evening was an atheist. She knew Minnie would be praying for him. She called Cathy, Johnny, and John into her tiny office to share the prayer need. John prayed as he taught the citizenship class. Cathy and Johnny remained there to pray. Lillian went on to her other duties.

When school was over that evening, Mike came to find Lillian. He was leading Minnie, and he was excited. "Mrs. Isaacs, I want to do this job. May I read to Minnie next Tuesday?"

"We'll see, Mike. Would you like to take that textbook back to the post to read ahead just in case?" Lillian asked as she pointed to the New Testament she had given him.

"Yes, I would," he replied. "I've got to hurry now. See you next Tuesday." He left with a spring in his step.

"Mrs. Isaacs," Minnie said when she heard the door close. "He is a good reader. I prayed for him like you said, And I'll pray for him all week—every day—and I'll tell Grandma Tucker and Aunt Elsie on the bus going home tonight. They'll pray too. He'll be a good teacher for me, and maybe he'll learn something for himself."

Mike was just one of many GIs who heard a witness of Jesus while attending activities at the mission.

One Fourth of July the Isaacs rounded up everybody who did not have something special to do. They loaded the mission bus and headed to a favorite picnic spot. They were several miles out of town when Lillian suddenly remembered the lemonade in the refrigerator at the mission.

"We just have to go back, John!" she exclaimed.

"We can't go back now. We'll just buy soft drinks or get water to make do when we get there," John replied.

Lillian insisted, "Who ever heard of a Fourth of July picnic without lemonade? We have to go back!"

"It's too late to turn around," John mumbled as the bus slowed down. "I think we can drink water," he continued as he found just the right spot to turn the bus.

As soon as they stopped beside the mission, Lillian started for the kitchen. At the same time a motorcycle roared into Lacey Street and stopped.

"Hey," called a booming voice. A tall thin guy walked toward Lillian. "Where you going? Somebody told me we'd be welcome over here on the Fourth."

"You are welcome," Lillian replied as she opened the mission door. "We're going on a picnic. Get on the bus." When she returned from inside with the huge container, the young man took the lemonade from her and said, "But I've got a buddy with me."

"Bring him, and hurry!" Lillian said as she almost ran.

"Park it and run!" shouted the young man to his friend. He motioned toward the bus.

The three boarded, and soon the happy crowd was moving toward the picnic again. The boys from the post became a part of the group from the start. They enjoyed the singing and the food. Long before the end of the day they were asking about the other activities at the mission. One later became a helper at the mission.

One of the first helpers for the mission was from the military community. As Flora Klepac read the *Fairbanks Daily News-Miner* one day, she came across a familiar name. Lillian Kirtland Isaacs had just arrived in Fairbanks with her husband, the pastor of the Native Baptist Mission. She called immediately to ask if Mrs. Isaacs knew a Lois, Martha, Fay, or Max Kirtland, her college friends. She discovered that Lillian was their sister. Flora and her husband, John, a soldier at Fort Wainwright, came to visit the Isaacs that day.

From the first visit in 1960 the Isaacs knew they had found friends. Lillian introduced the Klepacs to her friends, "Flora Klepac is the kind of person who can come in and take charge of a kitchen. She has prepared for and fed many people at my house. And John Klepac can do anything. He even preached for John Isaacs when he was needed, and he can repair anything that can break!"

John Klepac retired from the military and they moved. But the Klepacs returned to Alaska several times as volunteers. They took care of the mission while John and Lillian were outside. And once they were assigned by the Home Mission Board to work a short time in Kotzebue, up above the Arctic Circle. The short assignment stretched to two years. They patterned their work after the work at Friendship Baptist Mission. Old-timers at Kotzebue liked what was happening in their church, and hated to see these volunteers leave. "The Klepacs loved us and visited us and helped us grow a strong church," they said.

Military men and their families were drawn to the mission, especially the foreign-born wives. Many came to the English-Citizenship School, the Bible study, and the worship services. The mission also ministered to them in times of special need.

Ok was a military wife. She had a need she kept well hidden. She came to English classes with a Korean friend. They asked about the citizenship classes. When several other students came close, however, Ok said "I'm a citizen already."

The other girls discussed Ok, "She thinks she's better than we are. We don't like her."

John and Lillian visited Ok. She was cold and unfriendly. She did ask for a schedule of activities at the mission. "This is for my husband," she said.

The next Sunday her husband and her young son came with her to worship. "Come and see me again soon," she whispered to Lillian.

John and Lillian made another visit. This time Ok said, "I want to come study when no one else come. Nobody like me."

140

Ok did come alone for two or three mornings each week. Each time she would ask to have the door locked so no one could come in. "I don't want anybody to know I not smart." Both Lillian and John worked with her patiently and lovingly. They prayed for her. She seemed so lonely and unloved.

One day Ok did not show up for her lesson. The Isaacs checked her house, but no one was there. They asked the Koreans at school that night, but they shrugged their shoulders, "Who cares?"

Lillian was worried about Ok. As she woke during the night, she prayed for Ok. The next morning as she washed the breakfast dishes, God whispered to her, "Ok is in the hospital at Fort Wainwright. Go immediately to see about her." She put down the dish towel and dashed to John's study across the street at the mission.

"Can't we wait until visiting hours this afternoon?" John wanted to know.

"No. God has impressed me to go now."

They set out immediately. As they drove toward the hospital, they prayed, "God be with Ok and let us be a blessing to her."

As they walked into the hospital, the administrator met them saying, "I've had someone trying to reach you to hurry here to see Ok. She's confined in a straitjacket now, but she screamed all night. She kept saying 'I nothing, a nobody. Nobody love me. I want to see Isaacs!' We gave her many shots to quiet her. Someone has to stay close to her. Will you go in and talk with her?"

"Of course," John and Lillian said immediately. "We are not afraid. You pray for us as we go."

They hurried into Ok's room. Lillian leaned close to her ear. "Ok, we're here. Jesus loves you, and we love you too. If we get you out of the straitjacket, will you be quiet and listen?"

"Yes, yes!" Ok said through her tears.

The nurse removed the jacket and left the room. The Isaacs talked to Ok softly and lovingly. Then

John read to her, "Come unto me, all ye that labour and are heavy laden, and I will give you rest" (Matt. 11:28). They prayed for her and with her.

When she became calm, she said, "I lie, lie, lie to everyone. Can Jesus forgive me? Buddha not answer." Then Ok's desperate story poured out. She had told everyone she was a United States citizen, but she was not. She had been gone long enough from Korea to lose her Korean citizenship. She felt she was a nobody and belonged nowhere. Now her husband had orders to rotate again to Korea.

"I not go," Ok firmly stated. "I kill self first."

"But Jesus loves you. Let Him give you His peace. He can help you, Ok."

"I sure need help," Ok said sadly. "I believe you, but I not see Jesus. When you read the Bible, He talk in my heart. When you pray, He talk in my heart. I trust the best I can."

Then the Isaacs instructed, "You obey the doctors and nurses so you can go home. Jesus will help you. Come to class day after tomorrow. We'll study citizenship so you can pass the test."

Then John added, "Remember Jesus will help you. The order to Korea can be delayed if necessary." Lillian gave her one more hug, saying, "We'll see you in class day after tomorrow."

When they left, the nurse was amazed. "What did you say to her? She acts like she's in her right mind."

"Oh, she is," John assured her.

"Thank you for taking good care of her. God bless you," Lillian added as they left.

As they drove home, John and Lillian discussed the seriousness of what lay ahead. They had committed themselves, and God, to helping Ok. They prayed, "Oh God, we trust You to guide us as each call is made to help Ok become an American citizen. She is Your child. We are Your helpless children too. We claim Jesus' promise, 'If ye shall ask any thing in my name, I will do it' " (John 14:14).

Lillian spent the next day making calls to secure Ok's naturalization. First she called the Immigration and Naturalization officer in Anchorage. The director said he would send an officer for her test *if* the judge would set a date, *if* the Isaacs would prepare her, *if* the general would postpone the departure for Korea.

Then Lillian called Judge Taylor's office. He was in the "Lower Forty-Eight" on vacation. Because it was an emergency, his secretary gave Lillian his number. He readily agreed to set a date for the final hearing and asked Lillian to get the clerk of the court to set the hour. He gave his promise to be in Fairbanks for the proceedings.

Next Lillian called the general. He was most cooperative and agreed to delay the rotation date.

God had worked in many people to help Ok. Now He worked to give her a mind to learn. She was at peace with Him, and learned quickly.

Lillian's final call was to the editor of the local newspaper. He sent a photographer to make Ok's picture at the hearing.

This special hearing was an emotion-packed experience. Lillian asked the judge for the privilege of speaking.

"Only in America could this meaningful event take place. God had people write into our constitution the worth of the individual. Thanks to each of you for setting aside your busy schedules, Yes, thank you . . . for taking time to help make a new way of life possible for Ok. May America always recognize and cherish the worth of the individual. We believe Ok will be a good citizen. None of you looked at the expense of this day, but at the worth of one person. Thank you. May God bless you."

Then the judge asked John to close in prayer.

Military men and their wives seemed to sense the Isaacs were their friends. So did the military officials. The hospital administrator and other officers called them for help as well.

The phone rang at the Isaacs' home late one night. "Hello," Lillian answered sleepily.

"Mrs. Isaacs, this is Lt. McMichael at Fort Wainwright. There is a young woman who has locked herself in one of the rest rooms at her quarters here and is threatening to kill herself. She won't talk to us, but keeps asking for you. We are ready to break down the door, though she says she'll shoot herself if we do. Can you come?"

Instantly Lillian was awake. "Do you know her name? Do not break down the door! We will be there as soon as possible. Tell her we are coming."

When Lillian heard the girl's name, her heart sank. She was one of Liz Hall's students, but Lillian and John knew of her problems. They had visited with her a few days before. Lillian called Liz to go with her, and soon they were speeding toward the post.

As they drove, Lillian talked about their last visit with Marguerite. She had two children ages two and three, and had given birth to triplets three days earlier. Her husband had been ordered to report to the field. The situation seemed stressful, but Marguerite had seemed able to cope with it.

The Isaacs had read the Word to her husband. He had never made a profession of faith in Jesus. "That's a matter I ought to attend to," he said, after they told him of Jesus' love for him and the plan of salvation.

"Take this testament with you," John had said, "and ask Jesus to come into your heart."

"Thanks," the soldier had said, and tucked the little book into his pocket.

The car pulled up to the building where Marguerite had locked herself in the bathroom. A large crowd had gathered. An officer cleared the way for Lillian and Liz.

"She hasn't said anything for a long time. We

don't know if she's still alive. Shall we break down the door now?" the officer asked.

"No," said Lillian firmly. "Clear away the crowd as quietly and as quickly as possible. Tell any reporters there will be no statements until tomorrow. I'll go in to her."

"How will you get in? The door is locked."

"She'll open the door for me," Lillian assured him.

"But she has a gun! She might shoot you."

"She might shoot *you* if you break in the door, but she won't shoot me. I am her teacher."

The officer moved the crowd away. Lillian lay on the floor next to the door. Softly she called the girl's name. In the quiet, the dropping of a pin would have sounded like a cannon.

"Marguerite, Jesus loves you, and we love you."

"Ummm," sounded a low moan from the other side of the door. "Teacher?"

"Yes, Marguerite, we're here. Mrs. Hall is with me. We love you. No one will hurt you. Open the door."

In a moment there was a click. The door opened and a sobbing young woman fell into Lillian's arms. Marguerite's world had collapsed. Her husband had been killed in an accident immediately after arriving at his assignment. She could think of no way to cope with her life. Liz placed her arms around the sobbing girl and helped her walk down the hall while Lillian gave directions to the officer.

"Have someone take the older children for a few days. Get someone to look after the triplets tonight. Get someone else to sit with Marguerite, but let her sleep. No reporters until we get back tomorrow."

The officer followed Lillian's requests, and Liz and Lillian got Marguerite to bed. They reminded her of God's love and theirs. They assured her God could take care of every situation. They told her that her children were already in good hands. They convinced her to sleep and let God give her His peace.

145

Lillian and Liz worked with Marguerite for many days. They stayed close at hand until she was strong enough, with God's help, to stand alone.

Help between the mission and the military ran in both directions.

One day Lillian and John visited a military wife who had attended school only once, but who had expressed great interest. She was a young Korean mother named Ok Soon who could barely speak English. She was glad to see them, for she rarely got out of the apartment on the post. Her husband had field duty regularly each week. She was proud of her three children—all in diapers. The youngest was a newborn. The middle one, a daughter, was just 14 months old. Her oldest was a 4-year-old boy who had been injured at birth. Since he could not do anything for himself she, in reality, had three babies. Ok Soon had a great desire to learn English and to become a citizen.

"Is impossible," she said sadly. "Babies must have nurse. Husband in field when have school. I no learn. And no citizen."

John and Lillian assured Ok Soon that Jesus loved her, and that everything is possible with God. "Jesus loves you. He will help you, and we will help you."

When they returned home, Lillian went to see Ivy Brooks. She learned of government-supported facilities that would care for young children with birth injuries such as that of Ok Soon's oldest boy. Lillian discovered there was space and potential help available for the child. He must be brought every morning and picked up in the afternoon. He would not need to bring anything. His diapers, hot lunches, and activities would be provided by trained workers who would pattern him to strengthen his muscles. Hopefully he might even learn to walk and talk.

Transportation for the child seemed to be the only problem. Since the family lived at the post,

Lillian called the general's office. A young man answered, said the general was busy, and asked if he could help. Lillian explained the problem. He seemed unimpressed, and reminded her this was a military installation, not a family and children's agency. Her request for transportation was out of the question.

Lillian then hung up and looked in her book for the special number the general had given her. In less than a minute she was talking with Lieutenant Madden, the general's personal assistant, about the problem.

"Of course, we will transport the child to and from the center. Just tell me the times. You say Corporal Lufkin told you it couldn't be done? I'll just put that on his assignment sheet. It will be good for him to learn the army has a heart."

"Now, Mrs. Isaacs, what else can I do for you?"

Lillian could hardly believe all she was hearing, but she knew God had told her to call the general and he would help her. "There is one other thing, Lieutenant Madden. Would it be possible for the father of the boy to be out of the field and at home one night a week so his wife could come to school to learn English and citizenship?"

"Just tell me the night you want her," the lieutenant replied.

"Tuesday night is the regular night."

"His schedule certainly can be arranged. He will be assigned to his home on Tuesday nights to babysit. Is there anything else?"

"No, and I do thank you. God bless you for your kindness and your help, and give my regards to the general," said Lillian.

"Call this number any time, Mrs. Isaacs, any time."

With a prayer of thanksgiving, Lillian went back to her work.

Ok Soon attended school. She learned English and passed her citizenship test. When the time

147

came for her to be naturalized, she chose *Lillian* as a part of her new name. The officer asked her why she had added a non-Korean name to her own. Her answer told her story. "Lillian Isaacs is my teacher. She made possible for my son to go to school. There he learn to talk, to walk, to be regular boy. Now husband proud of son and wife. We somebody— good American now. My new name is Ok Soon Lillian Zellonos."

Each time Lillian talked with the general, he asked about Aunt Elsie and Grandma Tucker. One day a special messenger came to Lillian's house. The general had read a newspaper article about someone stealing Grandma Tucker's winter wood supply. "Mrs. Isaacs," the messenger said, "the general says to tell Grandma Tucker not to worry. She will have winter wood. He has assigned a truck and men to keep her supplied. If it ever looks a little low, you just let me know."

Not only the army, but the air force and the whole community of Fairbanks pitched in to help Grandma Tucker in this time of need. When the wood arrived, Aunt Elsie went to visit her. The two women stood in front of Grandma Tucker's tiny house and sang hymns of praise and gave thanks to God for His wonderful outpouring of love.

The story of the wood had become such news that the Associated Press came to take pictures for their world news service. With cameras poised, the photographers were ready to snap photographs of Aunt Elsie and Grandma Tucker as they sang beside the woodpile.

"No pictures," Aunt Elsie declared, "until after you say 'Praise the Lord.' "

At first the cameramen thought she was joking. They learned quickly that praising God was not a joke to these women.

"Praise the Lord," the men said rather weakly. Aunt Elsie was determined.

"Louder," she exclaimed.

"Praise the Lord," went forth a shout, followed by a burst of flashbulbs.

John talks with Grandma Tucker, a member of his congregation.

Lillian dressed for the cold Alaska weather.

13
Other
Dimensions

LEADERS of Tanana Valley Associational WMU came to Lillian for help. They wanted to continue their work with the literacy school, but they knew there were other needs in the community. They wanted Lillian's input. She suggested several projects, but cited one that caught the imagination of the group.

Many teenagers were confined in the Fairbanks jail. Surely they had needs the WMU could meet. Lillian was asked to serve on a committee with Rubye Thomas and Liz Hall to investigate the needs.

After much prayer, they made an appointment with the warden. He was cooperative, and wanted all the help the women could give. As the interview came to a close, he turned to Lillian and said, "You have my backing in any project you choose. I only ask that you come when you say you will." Directing his remarks to Lillian, he added, "You are in charge. I will help you any way I can."

"Oh, I am not in charge. I am not the chairman of the committee," Lillian protested.

"You are in charge *here*. What *you* plan we will

do." The warden stood. His visit was concluded. He had made his own appointment, and his contact person would be Mrs. Isaacs. The matter was closed.

The girls in jail were bored and sullen. There was absolutely nothing to do. There was no entertainment, no study, no magazines, no reading material—nothing. The matrons found discipline to be difficult, and morale low. Only brutal force could make the girls keep their cells halfway clean.

The WMU members prayed, and God directed. A contact with the girls was planned for one day each week. On Mondays, Rubye Thomas went to the jail and taught the girls hair care, hair styling, nail care, and fashion. Others helped her as she requested. The girls responded to her love and interest.

As their interest grew another program was added. Several seamstresses began a course in sewing on Saturdays. First, they taught the girls to embroider on pillowcases. As the girls worked, Lillian told stories from the Bible. Lillian collected the work at the end of the session and took it with her until the next week.

These pillowcases were to fill a special need. As the cases were finished, Lillian would take a needy person or a handicapped person with her to the jail to receive an embroidered gift. That giving was the first experience in sharing most of these girls had known. They had never seen nor heard people like Aunt Elsie, Grandma Tucker, or Blind Minnie. Each recipient thanked the girls for the gift, and gave a testimony about Jesus.

Tu, Ok Cha, Chin Sun, and others gave testimonies of how Jesus Christ had changed their lives. The girls responded to those who took time to come and share. They often cried as the visitor spoke. Many realized for the first time the value of their own homes and country.

Chin Sun reacted for all who had the opportunity

to go to the prison with John or Lillian. "Mr. Issacs asked me to go with them to prison. I not know why he asked *me*. I not important, but he made me feel special. I receive blessing."

Lillian began to read to the girls. The first book she read was *Tortured for His Faith* by Haralan Popov. They had never heard such a book. Many had never had anything read to them. They knew they were in jail for misdeeds; they found it hard to believe someone could be put in jail because he was a Christian, a good man. They liked the story. One girl asked to reread the book. Lillian loaned her the book and charged her with its safekeeping.

"She'll tear it up!" snarled the matron. "They've torn up every book they've ever had!" But the book was guarded and passed carefully to all who could read. Even the matron read it.

Because that book was well treated, others were shared. Finally Bibles were secured for the girls who wanted them. As books were enjoyed over the months, Lillian suggested the WMU start a small library.

Later, planned recreation was started on Tuesdays for both boys and girls. On Wednesdays John taught a brief Bible study or gave a Bible message. Thursday was music day. Eventually, there was a planned contact for every day of the week.

Something about the jail bothered the Isaacs. Many of the girls could not read. Few had finished school and even fewer had any real skills. Their release would leave them even more vulnerable to crime. They needed to be taught. As Lillian studied the situation, and prayed about it, she realized the need was too great to be handled by volunteers alone.

She knew what must be done. She made an appointment with the superintendent of schools. She pointed out the needs to him, and asked that a teacher be hired to teach at the jail. The superintendent could hardly believe such a need had never been called to his attention. Immediately he appointed a teacher to start an educational program for the prison. In a short time, the system employed two full-time teachers to hold regular classes there.

Many inmates, both boys and girls, were able to finish high school and begin vocational or professional training as a result of this program.

From the start, the girls felt free to write letters to Lillian. One letter brought strange results. It read, "Dear Mrs. Isaacs, The man who is responsible for what I have done is dead. He has committed suicide, but I had already forgiven him. Please go to his funeral and cry for me."

The girl gave the time and place of the funeral. Many persons were surprised to see the Isaacs at the funeral. One of the most surprised was a physician. When he asked why they came, they told about the young girl's letter. They told him of their work at the jail. When he asked further, they told him about their work with the Eskimos and the foreign born. As they talked the doctor wept. Then he asked them to pray for him.

As they started to leave, he said, "If I can ever be of any service to you, please call me. I will be happy to serve you."

This man became the Isaacs' family doctor. He had many opportunities to serve others as they called him on many occasions to serve the larger family of their ministry.

One year the busy fall season moved especially quickly to Thanksgiving. Christmas was approaching rapidly. As usual, a Christmas play was planned for the children and others at the mission. Lillian had written the play to include every person. Angels could be of any age, and so could shepherds. There could be angel choruses or shepherd choruses. Numbers were no problem. But they *did* have a problem.

The problem involved two brothers in the community who were faithful in attending activities at the mission. Lillian could count on Andy to take any part and do it well. His older and bigger brother was entirely different. The older boy was handicapped, so Andy was charged with his care. The older child was also a troublemaker. Both boys were often shunned because of his behavior.

The previous Christmas Lillian let both boys be angels. Somehow they made it through the performance. Now she had to find a way to help the older child so Andy would be allowed to come and be a part of the play. The handicapped boy had recently decided to take a stuffed animal with him everywhere he went. Under no circumstances would he be separated from this toy. It seemed the stuffed animal would have to be written into the play.

Johnny was now in high school. He always made scenery, gathered props, and designed costumes. This time, Lillian asked him to make plans for a sick lamb costume. He was also assigned to work with the WMU volunteers who furnished the costumes.

The last detail had been arranged. WMU volunteers had been enlisted to help with refreshments, programs, and gifts for the children. Everything seemed in order. After one more committee meeting the Isaacs could go home to get ready for Christmas Day.

As they crossed the street toward home that evening, Johnny announced, "I hope nobody else comes, Mama. I need you to help me decorate the Christmas tree."

"That's what we'll do right away, Johnny," Lillian promised, "after I tidy up the living room just a bit." But before she finished, she heard a knock at the back door.

"Come in, Mr. Aldrige. Merry Christmas!" Johnny heard his mother say.

"What's merry about it?" came a caustic reply.

154

"I haven't had a single card or gift. Nobody cares about me at all!" When Mr. Aldrige took off his lightweight coat and scarf, Lillian noticed he was thinner than when she saw him last. She suspected he did not have much to eat.

"Won't you eat some supper?" she asked, and wondered what she could offer. Even the ever-ready soup pot was empty.

"Well, I *am* hungry," he volunteered as he pulled up a chair to the table. Lillian opened a can of soup and made toast and tea. She also served cheese slices and fruit.

Mr. Aldrige was born in Germany. His family all lived in other places, and he was alone in Alaska. A fire had burned down his business. Then one day the truck he was driving broke down and he was stranded in the 40-below cold. By the time help came, his feet were frozen. The doctor had to remove several toes, and Mr. Aldrige knew he would limp the rest of his life. He was angry and bitter.

The Isaacs met Mr. Aldrige while he was in the hospital with frostbite. He was sarcastic when he spoke. He did tell them he lived in a trailer several blocks from the mission. Since the trailer had no running water, John invited Mr. Aldrige to come to the mission or to their house and take some fresh water each day.

Lillian saved empty bottles and plastic jugs for him to haul the water in. She made sure to fill them with piping hot water. The bottles gave him warmth as he carried them, but even so, sometimes he arrived at home with chunks of ice. Each time he came to the Isaacs' he sat down to eat what may have been his only meal for that day.

This particular evening John excused himself after dinner to put the finishing touches on his Christmas sermon. Christmas fell on Sunday this year. Johnny sighed as he left the room to decorate the tree alone. And Lillian was left with the angry, thin Christmas Eve visitor.

After listening to Mr. Aldrige's problems for about an hour, Lillian interrupted and tried to change the subject. "Don't you just love Christmas, Mr. Aldrige?"

"Why should I?" he scowled. His bitterness showed he thought of Christmas as one more burden he must bear.

"You do know why we have Christmas, don't you?"

"I certainly do not!" replied Mr. Aldrige.

"Well, I want to tell you a Christmas story—the real Christmas story," Lillian said. She reached for her Bible and turned to the account given by Luke. She read slowly and clearly about God's gift.

"This gift of Jesus is for you, Mr. Aldrige."

He mumbled some sort of response—softer and less belligerent than usual.

"And we want you to have Christmas dinner with us tomorrow right after church," Lillian continued as she helped Mr. Aldrige with his scarf.

When he was gone, she turned off the lights on the tree Johnny had decorated. For the first time she thought about Christmas dinner. "What in the world, Lord, will I feed Mr. Aldrige tomorrow? I don't even know what I'll give John and Johnny."

The answer came as clearly as the message did to the shepherds on that first Christmas night. "Fear not. Peace. I've already taken care of that. Get some sleep."

The telephone awakened the family early. "Lillian, this is Mary Lou Crawford. I've cooked dinner for a family of folks who can't come. Can you and your family eat with us after church?"

"Only if Mr. Aldrige can come. He's to eat with us today," said Lillian.

"Sure. The more the merrier," was the joyful reply.

"And Mary Lou, I know you have something to wrap for Mr. Aldrige so he will have some packages under the tree," Lillian added before hanging up the phone. Then, "Thank You, Lord," she breathed, and dressed for church.

The day was cold and snowy, but there was warmth in the heart of Mr. Aldrige as he sat around the Crawford's Christmas tree. The gifts were a surprise. He sniffed self-consciously and looked away from the others. The afternoon passed too quickly and the time came to leave to go to the final play rehearsal. Mr. Aldrige agreed to come to the Christmas play at the mission that evening. Before they left, the Isaacs thanked Mrs. Crawford for helping them have such a wonderful day and for helping Mr. Aldrige understand something of the Christmas spirit.

The sanctuary was filled. Not even one other person could squeeze into a seat. All characters were costumed and ready for their entrances. Even Andy's parents were present. Usually they showed no interest in the boys.

That night two of the angels sang a special song in Eskimo. The hush that followed created a feeling of awe and wonder about the scene forming in the center of the platform. Mary pulled the covering over her straight black hair and lowered her almond-shaped eyes to gaze into the manger. Joseph moved closer to her. Several shepherds—one of them pushing a larger shepherd who carried a sick lamb—knelt in reverence.

Then the other angels joined in a full and glorious chorus. "Glory to God. Peace on earth. Good will toward men."

The Spirit of God seemed to hover close.

Before he pronounced the benediction, John gave an invitation for any who wished to accept Jesus as Saviour. He explained carefully that Jesus came as a baby, but lived and died and rose from the grave to save lost people everywhere.

As the congregation sang, one small shepherd made his way to the preacher. "I invited Jesus to

157

be born in my heart tonight, Mr. Isaacs. And he was," Andy said when he placed his hand into John's.

The Isaacs declared the play a success!

On December 26, Maria Marchuck called from the Fairbanks hospital. "Good Jesus is here," she said by way of greeting. Then she continued, "George (her husband) had stroke yesterday, Christmas. Weather 50 below. Today we come in car to hospital for George. Boys go back home. I stay with you. Come in car."

Lillian understood.

Some missionary couples were stationed out in the villages where there were no hospital facilities. Before the birth of a baby the wife would spend the last weeks with the Isaacs. Or, if relatives were in the hospital, missionaries would make the Isaacs' home their home. Occasionally Eskimos or foreign born would do the same. Now Grandma Marchuck, as she was fondly called, would be their guest while her husband was hospitalized.

John went immediately to bring Grandma Marchuck home. When she came in, she blessed the doors and every part of the house. With her head on the floor she thanked God for the day, this home, the hospital, the Bible. On and on she prayed, thanking God. Although she included food in her thanks, she ate little. She kept her Bible close to her. She explained, "I separated from Bible once for many years. Want it near me now."

Grandma Marchuck stayed with the Isaacs for 31 days. During that time she set a routine for herself and for them. After she had prayed, she always said, " 'They that sow in tears shall reap in joy. He that goeth forth and weepeth, bearing precious seed, shall doubtless come again with rejoicing, bringing his sheaves with him' (Psalm 126:5-6). Gospel seeds must be watered with tears to grow. We must do something for Jesus today."

Every day, even before she visited George, she wanted to visit and witness to someone from Germany. "God let me be in a concentration camp so I remember the German people," she explained. As a young mother, she tried to flee communist Russia and was taken to a German concentration camp. There she met Betsie and Corrie ten Boom, and shared their flea-infested bed.

Each morning, Grandma Marchuck and Lillian prayed before they visited. Grandma said nothing during the visit, but continued to pray. Either John or Lillian would give a witness to the family. As a result several Germans came to know Christ as Saviour.

During the first week of Grandma Marchuck's visit, Lillian suggested, "Let's study citizenship while you are here."

"I tried before. I can't do it," Grandma Marchuck concluded sadly. She was now past 65 years of age.

"Don't you think Good Jesus can help you pass?" Lillian asked.

"I pray about it."

The next day, she began her 25-day study. When the study was over, George was much better and Grandma Marchuck took him home to Big Delta.

Later a notice came for her to take the citizenship test. She returned to the Isaacs'. They went to be with her and the other students from the school. Grandma Marchuck stood close to the Immigration and Naturalization officer's room and prayed.

The new officer called Lillian inside to help explain the proceedings. Then, he called Grandma inside also, so Lillian could demonstrate the testing. Later Grandma Marchuck told Lillian that she stood at the door as Good Jesus had told her to do. He revealed to her that Lillian would ask her the questions. Thus, Good Jesus had made it possible for Grandma to have her own teacher give the test she had dreaded. She passed with flying colors.

At the mission graduation ceremony, John introduced Grandma Marchuck to tell what becoming a citizen meant to her. Grandma stood beside John, but before she spoke she began to weep. She never uttered one word. A hush fell over the audience as she stood and wept and wept. Finally she went to her seat.

The program continued. Afterwards, as the group started to move noisily toward the basement, a clear beautiful voice was heard. Silence suspended the movement of the crowd. Grandma Marchuck was standing by the piano singing in her native Ukrainian tongue. Though the language was strange, no interpreter was needed for everyone to know she was singing a hymn of praise to God. The group exited quietly when Grandma Marchuck finished.

Later the Immigration and Naturalization officer told the Isaacs, "Her weeping was the most eloquent speech I have ever heard. She is a most unusual woman."

Lillian added softly, "She is the most Christlike person I have ever known."

Mr. Aldrige continued through the rest of the winter to come to the mission to get water and to wash his clothes. He could hang clothes in the furnace room where they would dry. The heat of the furnace kept him warm for the whole day. On laundry days he would have tea, a sandwich, and a bowl of soup at the Isaacs' home. Lillian still thought he did not have enough to eat for he looked thinner and thinner.

One day Mr. Aldrige mentioned that some nights he was too cold to sleep well. He would get the hot water late in the day and keep it close to his little heater. Then he would put it into the bed with him. As the night got colder and colder, the water would cool, then freeze. Mr. Aldrige would awaken encased in ice.

"You must sleep in the mission!" Lillian exclaimed. "There's room for you. We have plenty of blankets. The heat of the furnace will keep you warm."

"If it gets any colder, I may do that," Mr. Aldrige promised. But he never did.

His heart was touched as he visited the mission. At first he came just for the physical warmth. Once he sat with Lillian and listened to a gospel radio program. The preacher said, "You just need to give your heart to Jesus."

Mr. Aldrige put his head down on the Isaacs' kitchen table as though in prayer. Lillian heard him say through his tears, "I have done that."

At the mission he mended hymnbooks and Bibles, cleaned bookracks and dusted, and washed dishes or helped in the kitchen. In the spring he moved his work outside and cared for the grounds. He planted flowers along the sunniest side of the building and tended them with gentleness and love. Occasionally he would also mow the lawn or weed the garden at the Isaacs' house.

One day Mr. Aldrige was working in the Isaacs' yard. Andy came by to see Lillian that day. "Hi, Mr. Aldrige, the flowers sure are pretty today," Andy called.

Mr. Aldrige straightened up a bit, threw up his hand, and grinned at the boy.

"Hello, Andy. Come on in," Lillian said from the kitchen. She was busy cooking supper. Andy slid into a chair at the table and remained quiet. Lillian sensed this was not a regular cookie visit, so she dried her hands and took a seat across the table.

"Mrs. Isaacs, I've got a problem. Will you give me a birthday party?" Andy poured out his heart all at once.

"Oh," exclaimed Lillian in surprise. "You need a birthday party?"

"Yes, ma'am," he continued. "You see, last week I went to Frank's party. All the kids invite me to parties but my brother comes too and acts mean.

They say I never have had a party to invite them back, so they're never gonna invite me again."

"That is a big problem, Andy," Lillian said.

"Well, even worse, I said I was too gonna have a birthday party on my next birthday and they were all invited. And will you give me one—with a cake and all?"

Lillian thought a minute. "Yes, Andy, I'll give you a birthday party, and all your friends can come. You invite them," Lillian moved to continue her meal preparation.

Andy's face took on a glow that rivaled a fresh spring morning in Alaska. "Oh boy," he shouted as he hugged her around the waist and headed for the door. Suddenly he stopped, and his face fell. "Mrs. Isaacs, *we* still got a problem. My birthday is tomorrow."

Lillian caught her breath, but smiled as though she had nothing to do but plan birthday parties for little boys. "That's fine, Andy. The party will be ready at 4:00, cake and all, in the yard at the mission."

Lillian listened to Andy's delighted squeals all the way down the street. As she cooked she started to plan a party for the next day. She thought of Augusta Brown. She knew Augusta would help her bake a cake.

Lillian recalled the previous spring when she had visited Augusta Brown. Augusta needed to find a job, but had no real training. John and Lillian had offered her the job of cleaning the mission. She was thrilled and said it was an answer to her prayers.

Augusta cleaned and dusted with a real love for the One whose house she prepared. She carefully arranged flowers for the sanctuary. Her work was an act of worship for her.

Once Lillian went to the mission on Saturday afternoon. She thought Augusta had already gone home. She heard beautiful music coming from the piano in the sanctuary. When she investigated, she found Augusta playing as the tears streamed down her cheeks.

"Oh, Mrs. Isaacs," she said, "I didn't mean to disturb you."

"You didn't disturb me, Augusta. Go right ahead. I'm enjoying your music. I didn't even know you could play," Lillian said as she moved toward the door.

Augusta softly closed the piano. "I only play what I hear, and I only play for God. When everything is clean and ready, inviting and pleasing to Jesus, I just play a little and offer it to him."

After Sunday services, Augusta cleaned and set up the classrooms for school on Tuesday nights. Since she needed the work, Lillian also asked her to come to her house several mornings each week to help.

Lillian remembered how Augusta had laughed one morning as she put on the kettle and got the soup pot ready. "You know, Mrs. Isaacs, I've never been to your house when you didn't have tea and soup ready, like you were expecting someone to come." After she thought a minute she added, "I suppose when as many people drop in for lunch as come here, you do just always expect someone."

They laughed together as Lillian took ingredients for the soup from the pantry and the refrigerator.

"No meat today," commented Augusta.

"No meat today," Lillian smiled, thinking Augusta might not appreciate her meat secret. She was half tempted to tell how all during the winter she kept meat in the soup. She remembered the snowy day when she heard Champ barking for John to come out to play. When she went to the door, the snow was drifted almost to the rooftops all over the neighborhood. There stood Champ wagging his tail and pushing a package toward Lillian. He would bark, push the package, back off, and wag his tail. Finally, when Lillian picked up the package, Champ smiled and left before she could speak to him again.

163

When she took the package inside, she found a beautiful moose roast. She thought for a long time about this strange gift. Most likely Champ had jumped from the high snow right into somebody's winter meat supply. (During the cold season, many people kept their meat on the roof.) Then he had brought her a part of his find. At first she did not know what to do, but after careful consideration, she put the meat into the soup she was making, and said a prayer of thanks.

Often when there was a need to give food supplies to a needy family, Champ seemed to know. He would bring a piece of freezer wrapped meat, bark, push the package to Lillian, smile, and leave. Many times he had supplied meat for the soup that fed some of the hungry ones who came to the Isaacs' door. Since there was no way to trace the source of the meat to return it, Lillian just accepted it, and put it to good use.

That day, the snow had melted, and Champ could no longer jump to the roofs. The menu boasted vegetable soup.

The sight of Johnny through the window called her back to her present duties. Lillian thought, "I know that in the morning after we make soup, Augusta will help bake Andy a birthday cake."

"Hello, Johnny. I'd like you to help me with some birthday games tomorrow afternoon at 4:00 if you can. I'll tell you all about it at supper. Wash your hands now, and call your dad from the study, please. We'll be ready to eat in about five minutes."

Johnny was wise beyond his years. He laughed as he threw his books in a chair and said, "Mama, if I didn't know better, I'd say you are cooking up something besides supper!"

Birthdays were special to Andy. They were also big occasions in the Isaacs household. Cards and gifts arrived by mail from the Lower Forty-Eight, and family celebrations were scheduled around meetings and appointments. One day often was not enough time to celebrate. Usually the celebrations were stretched into birth month happenings.

Each birthday took its own significance, but certain years called for more elaborate celebrations. The year Johnny was ten and the September he was old enough to drive were such times.

John's 65th birthday was one of the most important for the entire family. Johnny was a senior in high school. John and Lillian had prayed and thought a long time about what to do when this birthday arrived.

They decided John would retire after this birthday, but Lillian would still work. The Home Mission Board had asked her to become a literacy missionary. Her territory would be the United States as a whole. Based in one city, she would travel wherever she was needed to teach in workshops, to promote literacy missions, and to inspire people to respond to the need for literacy workers. God assured Lillian this job was right for her. She also knew God had special plans for John. John learned quickly that retirement meant simply shifting gears in the Lord's work.

Lillian visits with Augusta Brown, member of Friendship Baptist Mission.

Florida Footprints
(1972-)

14
To the Lower Forty-Eight

IS THIS the way parents send a son off to college?" Johnny asked as he looked at the packing crates and boxes that surrounded them.

"Well, no, not exactly, Johnny," Lillian replied. "Most folks don't pack all of their belongings as well as those of the prospective student—and then go with him when he leaves."

"It's good that Augusta is helping us or we'd never make it!" Johnny added, as he heard her familiar knock at the back door.

"You're right! Come in, Augusta! We were just being thankful for you. You can start packing in the kitchen with the dishes while I pack John's books. Johnny, you start with your things— clothes, anything you want for school, records, books. Everything has to go, or be disposed of."

The three worked for several days to have the freight ready for shipment. They left out just enough clothes and souvenirs to fill the suitcases that would be taken on the plane as they flew to Florida.

Lillian remembered the trip from Kentucky to Fairbanks in 1960. "How did we get all of our junk in that little trailer? How could we have collected so much more junk to haul away?" She remembered the house as it stood furnished and ready for them. She wanted to leave it the same way.

John, blissfully unaware that packing was taking place, continued to minister to members of the mission and to people in the community. Several farewell dinners and parties were given those last few weeks in Alaska.

All of Fairbanks seemed to sense the vacancy the Isaacs' leaving would create. Religious, military, and civic leaders alike reflected on the contributions of one family to the quality of life they enjoyed in their city.

The Borealis Kiwanis Club presented John a special citation as Minister of the Year. Citations from the United States Immigration and Naturalization Service, Alaska's court system, the President of the United States, and the office of Alaska's Governor Egan were among commendations given. The general at Fort Wainwright also gave a citation thanking the Isaacs for their help to his men and their wives.

Lillian packed the citations and commendations in the box with her Woman of the Year award, Johnny's high school diploma, and other such memorabilia. Then she moved on to finishing the job at hand.

The Fairbanks *Daily News-Miner* gave a good summary of the Isaacs' reaction. "At the testimonial dinner a whole table was set aside for gifts, plaques, and citations honoring the couple.

"To the unassuming John and Lillian Isaacs, however, the real reward for their dozen years in Fairbanks is knowing that the work is continuing."

The mission family had their own good-byes— some as a family together, some privately. All dreaded the October departure day.

At last, that day arrived. The Isaacs left one field, and the next day found themselves on another.

15
New Desk and Pulpit

AGAIN the family stood surrounded by boxes. But this time they were in Tallahassee, Florida.

The phone rang. "Mrs. Isaacs, we need a substitute teacher for our seminary extension class. Do you think Mr. Isaacs will be free to do this for us?"

"He's standing right here. Why don't you just talk with him about it?" Lillian replied as she motioned for John to come to the phone.

John was thrilled with this new opportunity. He and Lillian knew God had again placed them where He wanted them to serve. They began to feel at home. Johnny enrolled at Florida State University. Lillian successfully completed her first assignment as a literacy missionary. John settled into his teaching routine for seminary extension.

Early in the year, John also began to teach citizenship to students in the program for internationals at First Baptist Church, Tallahassee. The English classes and literacy work had been in progress for about eight years. Mrs. John Wheeler, "Miss Martha," was director of the school. She was pleased to find a qualified citizenship teacher for those students who also needed to become citizens. Enrollment in the class was small, but John was not discouraged.

Among his early students was a young Korean woman named Naomi. John began the first session by saying, "Naomi, did you know that you have a Bible name?"

When she gave a negative reply, he told her the story of the great faith of Naomi. He concluded by asking, "Would you like to see that story in the Bible? And see your name there too?"

"Yes," she answered quickly.

"Would you like to have a Bible?" John asked.

Again Naomi answered, "Yes."

The next week John called to be sure Naomi would be at class. When he gave her the Bible, she asked for a hymnbook. The request was granted. John gave an invitation, "Come to church next Sunday. We have good teachers to help you understand. You will learn and hear more English."

John found a way to get better acquainted with each student and meet individual needs. With Maria, another early student, meeting the real need was quite difficult.

Maria was from the Azores. John told her, "You need to read better." She did not seem to understand what he was saying. "My wife will come to see you this afternoon and help you understand about our literacy program here."

At lunch John said, "Lillian, you must visit Maria. I told her you would be there at 4:00. She needs to learn to read. I'll drop you off while I go to the hospital, and pick you up in about an hour." Lillian went to visit, but she had a strange feeling as she watched John drive away.

Maria welcomed Lillian into her home, but not as a reading teacher. "I no want to learn to read! Want to learn citizenship!"

Lillian approached the problem from every side: learn to read to pass the citizenship tests; learn to read to be a useful citizen; learn to read to read the Bible; learn to read because the book is interesting. Maria refused to try. She only wanted to learn citizenship.

Lillian looked at her watch. She still had 50 minutes until John would come back. "Well," she said "let's study citizenship."

"All right!" Maria said with interest.

"Let's pray and ask God to help us," Lillian said. Then she uttered one prayer which Maria *and* God could hear, and one prayer that only God could hear. "Lord, what am I going to do with her?"

When the prayers were finished, Lillian had the answers. She took out a dollar bill which she had slipped into her pocket earlier in the day. "Maria, you can learn much about citizenship from this bill. First, you see the national motto, In God We Trust. It is on all United States money. Learn it, for the officer will ask you that question on your citizenship test."

Maria repeated after Lillian, "In God We Trust. I trust in You, God."

"This man is George Washington. He was our first president. You will be asked that question also. George Washington. Say his name."

"Georgie Washington," Maria said. "First president."

"George Washington," corrected Lillian.

"That what I say, Georgie Washington. In God We Trust." Lillian continued, leaving well enough alone. "Now turn the bill over. Here we see the history of mankind's search for freedom. It was first in the mind of God. You see His all-seeing eye. Hold it any direction. The eye still looks at you." Maria tried this, and nodded her head in agreement. Lillian continued. "That's because God is everywhere. You see light coming from the eye because God is light." Lillian pointed out each symbol on the bill, explaining each in a Christian light.

When she had finished, she added "Now in

which room do you spend the most time?"

"Kitchen," replied Maria.

"Where do you stand? At the table? At the stove? At the sink washing dishes?"

"Yes," Maria finally said.

"Good. I will write the motto on this card, and we will place it in the window so you can see it and practice saying In God We Trust. I want you to talk to God and tell Him you do trust in Him," instructed Lillian.

They moved to the kitchen. "Do you like to wash dishes? No? Well, you can say the motto, and thank God for many things. For each finger, for head, feet, for each member of your family, for your neighbors. Talk to Him. And next week when I come again, you will know this motto."

When Lillian returned the next week, Maria ran to the car to meet her. "In God We Trust. I trust in You, God." she said as she beamed at her teacher.

The lesson went well, and when Lillian started to leave, she asked, "Maria, do you go to church?"

At first Maria evaded the question, but she finally said, "No."

Lillian invited her to go to church the next Sunday. "Miss Martha will come for you. When her car rolls up to your door, go out and get in. Don't make her wait. You will sing, study the Bible, pray, and listen to the preacher. If you do not understand, you can talk to God. You can thank Him for the preacher, for the person on your right side and on your left side. There'll be lots of people there. You can pray for every one of them. I'll see you there." When Lillian got home, she called Martha to tell her she had been volunteered to bring Maria to church.

At the next lesson, Maria said with excitement, "I love to go to churchie! But I didn't get finished talking to God."

"Well, you may go again this Sunday," Lillian

said as they settled down for the lesson.

Maria finally became convinced that she must take the reading course in order to pass the citizenship test. She became willing to learn. After much studying she did pass the test for citizenship. She became a citizen of the United States, but better, she became a Christian.

Each week, Lillian made refreshments for the students in the seminary extension class. When she was out of town on assignment, she called on fellow church members Martha and John Wheeler to take her place. They filled in and did a good job. John Wheeler liked the class so much that he finally joined as a student.

As the first semester of seminary extension drew to a close, John and Lillian met with the dean, Rev. Lofton, to make plans for an end-of-the-semester banquet. Rev. Lofton mentioned that the school seemed unable to get much publicity about the banquet and its other activities.

"We must pray about that, Brother Lofton. Let's pray about it now," Lillian suggested. Together they brought the situation before God and asked for his solution.

When the prayertime was over, Lillian started toward the phone. "I'll go call the editor of the paper now."

"You'll what?" exclaimed Rev. Lofton.

"I'll call the editor. We prayed. I believe God expects us to act also." Lillian turned to the number in the directory. She found it and called the editor-in-chief of the local daily. Lillian introduced herself and explained what they wanted. "Mrs. Isaacs, I'll put you in touch with one of my best editors, Mr. Ecks. He will see that everything you bring in will be in print. If you would like a picture, bring that too."

When Lillian returned to tell about the successful

call, there was another prayertime to give thanks for God's answer.

The first banquet was held on Wednesday night during the family night supper hour at First Baptist Church. The pastor, Dr. Robert M. McMillan, greeted the group. The next day Rev. Lofton's picture appeared in the daily news with the article about the school.

Before the end of the second semester, John and Lillian had thought of several ways to point up the importance of the banquet. They also thought of ways to strengthen the ties between the school and the hosting church. Working with the WMU director at First Baptist, Lillian saw the accomplishment of both of those objectives.

The Acteens and older Girls in Action began to make place cards and favors with Bible verses on them. Members of Baptist Women and Baptist Young Women made lovely fresh flower arrangements for each table. The WMU director arranged to have linen cloths for the table. The dietician and kitchen staff served the group a special menu banquet style. The church and the pastor showed justifiable pride in their part in magnifying the teaching of God's Word through seminary extension.

John and his seminary extension class in Tallahassee, Florida.

16
Coast to Coast and Beyond

LILLIAN became accustomed to traveling a great deal. She conducted workshops and promoted literacy missions from coast to coast. She served as the inspirational speaker for associational and annual WMU meetings in several states, and was scheduled regularly for WMU and home missions conferences at Glorieta and Ridgecrest. Acteens learned to love her, and requested she be a speaker at each National Acteens Convention. She and John both spoke regularly for world missions conferences. Lillian's calendar stayed crowded, even during weeks marked for vacation.

When the Foreign Mission Board realized the importance of literacy as a tool for their missionaries, they turned to the Literacy Missions Department of the Home Mission Board for help. That Board invited Lillian to help Mildred Blankenship plan and hold their first workshop. Given as a part of new missionary orientation, the workshop was a success and has been continued.

Also, the Home Mission Board began providing an intense training course in literacy each year. Lillian was heavily involved from the beginning.

Literacy workers from all over the Southern Baptist Convention came for advance training and to study new and developing methods of decoding the printed page for nonreaders. They enjoyed hearing Lillian speak and received inspiration from her. Eventually, the inspirational messages of each session became her chief responsibility. Others, some she had trained, took over the task of teaching.

On each of Lillian's trips, John had a definite assignment to do while she was gone. "Pray for me as I go, John. Pray that God will let me be a blessing to someone," Lillian requested. They still operated as a team.

In 1979, Lillian and Mildred Blankenship went to Hawaii to promote literacy missions. One night Lillian awoke with chest pains and difficulty in breathing. She realized her help must come from God. She prayed for freedom from pain and ease in breathing.

Peace and assurance came to her as she heard Him whisper, "Don't be afraid. I will take care of you, and you will be all right. Continue My work here as planned." Then He told her exactly what to do to feel better. "You must eat lightly, rest when you can, sleep propped up in bed. Go to the doctor immediately when you get home."

Lillian and Mildred finished the work in Hawaii and returned home. Within a few days Lillian saw a heart specialist. He was alarmed when he heard the gurgling sound that Lillian had listened to continuously for the last weeks. He called in a surgeon to consult with him on Lillian's case.

"Mrs. Isaacs, you have a severe problem. You may have had it since birth, but now it is critical. We must do open-heart surgery immediately."

In the few days before her surgery, Lillian thought of the times as a child when she just could not run fast like the other children did. She remembered as a young woman lying on the floor to try to make the pain in her chest go away. And she

178

remembered her severe illnesses in Kentucky.

John and Johnny prayed as they never had prayed before. Then John said, "Sweet, you are not to worry. God will take care of you."

They talked together of the time in Alaska when they received the message that their Kentucky friend, John Arrington, had suffered a heart attack. When the Bible study group met at the mission, Aunt Elsie said, "Give me somebody to pray for especially today."

"Pray for John Arrington in Kentucky. He's had a heart attack," John said.

The next day, Aunt Elsie came again with the same request. "Give me somebody to pray for especially today."

"John gave you the name of John Arrington yesterday. Pray for him," Lillian reminded her.

"I prayed for heart-attack-John yesterday when I got home. God hear me and say he be all right. Give me another name."

Lillian had been curious about Aunt Elsie's answered prayer, and asked what time it was when God told her her prayer was answered. Aunt Elsie gave the time. Later Lillian checked with the Arrington family to discover that at the time Aunt Elsie had given, John Arrington had been able to move from the oxygen tent.

"We need to let some of our praying friends know we need their prayers now," they said. Within a short time, people all over the States were joined in praying for God's will to be done in Lillian's life.

Ok Cha Taylor expressed the feelings of many. "Mrs. Isaacs sick? Her heart? She can have my heart. I give it to her gladly."

God had further need of the Isaacs team. He guided the doctors as they replaced a valve in Lillian's heart. Then He healed her and strengthened her body as she rested. He sustained family members who sat with her around the clock and kept her household running smoothly. He upheld and comforted John and Johnny.

After the surgery, Lillian had to accept a different lifestyle. She had to have two hours of bed rest each day and had to exercise properly. With a few limitations, however, she could return to work.

The literacy work grew and prospered. The Board saw the need to divide the states and secure another worker. Lillian's territory was now smaller. She became responsible for literacy work in the states east of the Mississippi and Alaska.

Lillian ponders a question on literacy missions.

Lillian speaks to a group about literacy missions (1976).

Lillian (left) and Ethel Golden on a return visit to Kentucky.

17
Another Day

THE summer sun was already beating down on the front lawn. John hurried out to pick the green beans from his garden before even the shaded backyard and garden were too hot.

"I think we'll have enough beans to share with the folks next door. And I won't be too long picking with this heat," John said to Lillian.

Lillian moved toward the sink with some of the breakfast dishes in her hands. "Sounds good, John. I'll have everything ready and put lunch on the stove early."

As she started to wash dishes, she caught sight of a slight movement beyond the front fence. Then she saw Billy glance quickly from side to side, slip through the gate, and dart toward the front door. He popped into the kitchen and plopped into the red chair.

"Billy, would you like some lemonade?" Lillian asked.

Billy's eyes lifted in surprise, "You know it."

He sipped the cool lemonade and said a verse he had chosen and learned as a surprise for Lillian.

"That's a wonderful surprise, Billy! And a

wonderful verse! Thank you!" Lillian said, but Billy was busy finishing his lemonade, and did not look at her. Then he was gone, as quickly as he came.

As Lillian returned to the dishes, she mused on what a long way her relationship with Billy had come. She had seen the dirty, neglected child many times, and had described him as "a noise with dirt over it." He was constantly in trouble at home and in the neighborhood.

Her heart had gone out to him.

One morning as the noise passed her window, Lillian prayed, "Lord, I know You love Billy. How can I help him?"

"Teach him My word," the Lord answered.

"Lord, I can't even catch him. How can I teach him Your word?"

Suddenly Billy stopped. He seemed to be listening to something. He turned around, came straight to the Isaacs' gate, opened it, and walked to the steps. Lillian was there to meet him. "Hello, Billy."

No reply.

"Billy, God loves you. This is God's Word." She showed him the Bible she held. "I'm going to teach you a verse from this book that tells that He loves you."

"For God so loved the word that he gave his only begotten Son . . ."

"Say that again," Billy demanded.

Lillian repeated the verse, then helped him try to say it. Billy practiced, and soon he said it perfectly. Almost as suddenly as he had appeared, the seven-year-old was gone—to school or to play or to kick a can down the street and disturb the neighbors.

The next day, Billy came to the Isaacs' steps again. He said his verse perfectly. Lillian was as thrilled as he was.

"That's wonderful, Billy. I'll teach you another verse." This time she had chosen Psalm 34:7. Billy learned the verse quickly. He seemed to understand when Lillian explained what it meant.

Every day Billy came, and every day he learned a new verse. One day he confided, "I didn't sleep so good last night. I was skeered."

"You were? What frightened you, Billy?"

"Them ghosties at my house. Ever since Grandpa died, they come every night. They hit the walls and rattle things. I get so skeered I roll up in a ball and shake."

"Well, Billy," Lillian advised, "tonight when the ghosts come, you say your verses. And they will leave."

The next day Billy gave a happy report. "You were right. Them ghosties sure don't like my verses. I said 'em just like you told me to, and them ghosties took right out of there. I slept all night."

Another day Billy complained, "I don't like school! Nobody likes me, and the teacher hates me! She said I was the meanest child in the class."

"Billy," Lillian asked gently, "do you listen to the teacher as she explains the lesson? Do you try to help her instead of talking all the time? If you do your best, your teacher will like you."

Billy did not answer. He just sat still and quiet.

All too soon Billy brought the news that his family was moving away. By now he knew many verses and felt comfortable in the red chair at Lillian's kitchen table. His face and hands were clean and his hair was combed.

Lillian spoke gently. "Today I'm going to tell you the most wonderful story you'll ever hear. I've been telling you God loves you. He loves you so much that He sent Jesus to die for you. If you trust Jesus, you will go to be with Him forever when you die."

"I know that. What am I s'pose to do about it?" Billy asked.

"Just tell Jesus you're sorry for your sins and ask Him to come into your heart."

Billy confided, "Why, I already done that. I thought you knew. I asked Jesus to come in, and

He just slid right on down there." He pointed to his heart.

"No, Billy, I didn't know," smiled Lillian. "But that's great!"

"Know what? My teacher likes me now. She lets me say my verses to her. The other day she said, 'Billy, I don't know what's happened to you. Now you're the nicest boy in the class.' I didn't tell her my secret, but that's it, ain't it?"

They talked about the difference Jesus makes in a life. Lillian reminded him to keep saying his verses when he moved away.

A few months later Billy and his family returned to Tallahassee and the verse visits resumed. Whenever Billy came, Lillian stopped her work to listen and to teach him.

One Sunday morning Billy showed up dressed for church. Since Lillian was away Johnny took him.

"What are we doing now?

"Who's the man talking?

"What are they passing around to everybody?

"Why are they taking money? Do you have to pay to come to church?

"Huh! I can say my verses better than the preacher."

Worn and exasperated, Johnny brought Billy home immediately after the service. Later Lillian asked Billy how he liked Sunday School. "Not too much," he reported sadly. "You told me we'd study the Bible, but they colored instead. Couldn't even color too good. I said my verses for 'em, and one boy said he was glad I came!"

Billy did not return to Sunday School, but he continued to learn the Scriptures. He found verses on his own and brought them to Lillian as surprises. For one so young he had a keen understanding of what he read. Finally Billy stopped coming, but the difference in him was noticeable wherever he went. Instead of a noise with dirt on it, he was becoming the beautiful person God had made him to be.

185

Before the dishes were finished, John was back with the beans, and seeing the empty glass at the table, he said, "I thought I saw Billy coming toward the house. Got any more of that lemonade? It's already hot outside!"

Lillian poured another glass of lemonade, finished the dishes, and washed the beans. While John delivered some of his garden produce to the neighbor next door, Lillian prepared the rest of lunch, including the beans.

She was gathering her study material when John returned and took his place nearby to study. A few minutes passed in silence.

"John," Lillian announced as she put down her work and started toward the door, "Let's go to the hospital to see Max."

John continued to flip pages in his book looking for a good stopping place. "Wouldn't a little later do just as well?"

"No," Lillian insisted, "let's go now."

As they drove to the hospital, they remembered how they had met Max Cupit and his wife, Faye. The Saturday before Easter many years earlier, Lillian had stopped at the candy store in the mall.

"Easter is wonderful, isn't it!" Lillian remarked to the saleswoman.

"Oh, yes!" she replied.

Lillian added, "It makes me sad to see so few reminders of the real meaning of Easter."

The saleswoman agreed.

"I have a beautiful Easter story I'd like to give you," Lillian said as she reached into her purse.

The woman smiled and Lillian added, "Hope you get to go to church tomorrow."

"Maybe. My husband, Max, is a steward in the Methodist church, and sometimes I go with him. I used to go all the time, but with work and all, I don't get to go often now."

The next week Lillian stopped at the candy store again. "How did you like the Easter story?"

"I liked it. It made me think of the real meaning of the day."

"Would you like another—about the 11 appearances of Jesus after the Resurrection?"

Faye Cupit took the pamphlet. She seemed glad to have something interesting to read and glad to have found a new friend.

Lillian's literacy work took her out of town, and two weeks passed before she returned to the candy store. Faye had begun to wonder if she'd see her new friend again. When she saw Lillian come through the door, she rushed over to greet her and to ask about her absence. This gave Lillian a chance to tell her a little about how churches can get involved in teaching people to read.

"I really do miss my church," Faye explained. "I used to be active in Sunday School, and in the women's work, but I've lost out. My husband, Max, has cancer. He's going to the hospital to have a lung removed."

Lillian reached into her purse. "Take him this Bible, and tell him my husband and I will pray for him. Would it be all right if we come for a visit?"

The operation was successful. When John and Lillian visited Max, he told them that reading the Bible had brought back happy memories from his childhood. He said those memories were speeding his healing.

On one of their daily walks, John and Lillian discovered that Max and Faye lived less than a mile from them. The Cupits insisted they come in for Bible reading and prayer. This visit was the first of many.

Max became ill again and needed additional surgery. He asked John to come to pray for him. John asked, "Are you trusting Jesus? Has He forgiven your sins? Are you ready to go live with Him?"

To all of these questions, Max answered, "Yes." Then he added, "Since you sent the Bible, I have read it and trusted in Jesus."

187

For a while Faye continued to work. Lillian supplied Faye with tracts which she gave to her customers. But Max grew worse, and Faye retired early to stay with him. Each time John and Lillian visited Max in the hospital they brought a large piece of cardboard with a Bible verse written on it. Lillian propped it up on the table so Max could see it from his bed. As he read, he seemed to draw comfort.

The Isaacs were brought back to the present as they drove into the hospital parking lot. When they entered his room, Max asked, "What is my verse for today? I was looking for you. All of my friends are here."

Lillian stood the verse card on the table. "This is the day which the Lord hath made; we will rejoice and be glad in it" (Psalm 118:24).

Max read the verse several times and commented on its truth. He described the banquet table he saw, the guests around it, and the beauty of the other world he was glimpsing. "Get Faye from the kitchen. The banquet is ready. This is the best day of my life!"

John and Lillian left after assuring Faye that they were only a phone call away. They had been home only a few minutes when the phone rang. Max was gone. They returned to the hospital to drive Faye home, and to assure her of their love and help.

After two trips to the hospital in one day, John and Lillian were tired. They napped and then took their daily walk.

John and Lillian make it their custom to walk a mile each day. They make the time count for the Lord. Their route winds through the neighborhood where they live, and they minister as they go. Waving hands have replaced the cold silent stares that greeted them on their first walk. Even the dogs wag their tails in a friendly way when John talks to them.

They stop for at least one visit along the way. Some visits are long and some are short. Each includes a Scripture passage and a prayer.

One afternoon, they prayed, "Lord, let us find somebody to help today as we walk." About midway through their walk, they heard a shout. "Hey. Hey you!"

Not recognizing the voice, they walked on. It came again. "Hey there. I'm hollering at you!"

They turned to see a short, stout woman waving her arms and shouting. "You! You come here!"

When they reached talking distance, she asked, "Will you let me walk with you? My doctor wants me to walk, and I don't want to walk by myself."

Mrs. Roney became a regular walking partner. After each walk she invited John and Lillian into her home to read the Bible and pray.

One night as John and Lillian were about to leave for an all-night prayer retreat, the phone rang. Mrs. Roney's 12-year-old granddaughter spoke hurriedly, "Grandmother has to go to the hospital. Something is wrong with her heart. I've called my aunt and the ambulance. Here it comes now! Please pray!"

At the prayer retreat, Lillian requested prayer for Mrs. Roney.

"You go and check on her," the women said. "We will continue to pray."

Mrs. Roney stabilized at midnight. Lillian called the church and asked the women to pray all night for her.

The next day, to the doctor's amazement, Mrs. Roney was much better. In a few days she returned home. When John and Lillian came to visit, she asked them to read the verse in Hebrews about Jesus tasting death for every person (Heb. 2:9).

As they walked some days later, Mrs. Roney said, "You know the night I had the heart attack I tasted death. My doctor was there, and I was gone to the other side. My doctor called, 'Open your eyes!' The nurse was rubbin' my wrist. I looked at 'em and I could see 'em, but I could see Jesus too."

"What time did that happen?" Lillian wanted to know. It was the exact time the women had started praying.

"I knowed prayer was being made for me, and that He wasn't through with me. I know too that He tasted death for me, and He took the sting out of it. I tasted it myself, and someday I'll stay in that world with Him," declared Mrs. Roney.

Mrs. Roney had to return to the hospital for more surgery. Again John and Lillian prayed with her. After the surgery, she reported, "I had the greatest sense of peace come over me. I kept praying to Jesus. I heard an angel speak, 'Don't be afraid. Jesus is with you.' Ain't nothing like them angel voices!" she exclaimed. "They're next to Jesus. But Jesus' voice is first. I know 'cause I heard 'em both."

The day Max died they prayed for Mrs. Roney as they passed her house, but they did not stop. John had to teach the seminary extension class that night and Lillian had to put the finishing touches on the refreshments.

Later, John sat in his favorite chair and thought about all that had happened during the day. " 'This is the day that the Lord hath made.' "

"Yes," agreed Lillian. "We can thank God for many blessings today and for the life Max lived. We can ask for strength for Faye. And don't forget Billy and Mrs. Roney."

18
Christmas 1983

CHRISTMAS has always been one of the happiest times of the year at the Isaacs' house. In 1983 excitement started early.

Mildred Blankenship from the Home Mission Board came to visit for a few days. One morning as they lingered to chat over another cup of coffee, the phone rang. Lillian answered, and talked for a while trying to comfort someone. After hanging up, she said, "I must go to the prison at once and take a Bible. Our friend has a relative who has just been sent there, and she is distressed about him. She wants him to have a Bible."

Coffee conversation stopped. Johnny spoke up. "Mama, you can't just walk into a federal penitentiary like that. You'll waste hours, and may never get to the boy. If he just got there, he may be in restricted quarters. Here, give me the Bible. I'll take it." Turning to Mildred, he explained, "Since I teach reading in the school there, I already have identification and keys. Everybody knows it's OK when they see me walking into a cell block with a book."

"Thanks, Johnny," Lillian said as she gave him

a Bible. "Angels go with you."

"I might just do some more shopping anyway. I can stop at the mall on the way back."

As he started toward the door, Lillian stopped him. "Johnny, don't stop at the mall. I feel strongly that you need to come directly home."

"But, Mom," Johnny started to say.

"Come straight home, Johnny. It's important."

Lillian returned to the table for a last cup of coffee with Mildred and John.

As always John opened the Bible, all joined in prayer, and John sang an amen. The day was well under way.

While Lillian made preparations for lunch, the phone rang again. She heard John answer.

"Hello." Pause. "No, I'm sorry he's not here." Another pause. "No, I don't know when he'll be back."

By now Lillian had interrupted on the kitchen phone. "Excuse me, are you wanting to look at some of Johnny's paintings? He will be back in about an hour. Yes, you may come then. He will be happy to see you."

For the next hour the household waited anxiously to see if the artist and the art lover would arrive at the same time. Artist Johnny came in first.

"Mama, as I came by the mall, I felt a pull to go in. I really wanted to finish my shopping. But I remembered you said, 'It's important to come straight home.' "

"Someone is coming to look at your paintings. And I believe I hear him knocking at the door."

Lillian welcomed the caller, his wife, and his five-year-old son. They all began to look at Johnny's art. The child seemed most interested and asked Johnny all sorts of questions. Johnny tried to satisfy his curiosity. As the adults continued to talk, however, the little boy grew restless. Lillian took him to the kitchen for refreshments, and the mother followed. When the child began to read words he saw on their Christmas cards, Lillian gave him a stand-up folder that carried a part of the Christmas story from Luke. She saw immediately that he could read that too.

"Would you like to stand here by me and read that story aloud to me?" The little visitor stood close and read the verses on the folder.

"That story comes from the Bible. Would you like to read the whole story from the Bible?" Lillian asked.

The child nodded, and he read well. Lillian turned to his mother who had listened quietly. "How long has he been reading?"

"Since he was three."

Lillian turned back to the boy. "You read so well. You have thrilled my heart. I am going to give you this Bible for your very own. You have read many stories, but this book tells the greatest story of all. I want you to read it every day." His little hands eagerly took the Bible. It was his first.

"And I'm going to give you enough folders to put one at every place for your Christmas dinner. How many will you need?"

The little boy told about his older brother who would be at dinner.

"Does he have a Bible? No? Well, would you like to take one to give to him? Then you may. Tell him about this wonderful story, and tell him to read this book every day."

"Thank you, Mrs. Isaacs. I'll tell him, and we will read every day."

By now the father had made his purchase and was ready to leave.

"I have a Christmas present for you before you leave," Johnny said to the little boy. "It is a book that my mother wrote about a woman in Alaska. She was over 100 years old when she learned to read. I drew the pictures for the book."

After the boy and his parents left, Johnny reported that the young prisoner was glad to get the

Bible. He seemed eager to read, and was open to any message given by someone who cared about him.

The day after Mildred left, Lillian's brother, Max, and his family came for their Christmas visit. Maria also came for her regular Christmas visit. Her employer drove her over and also stayed to chat with the Isaacs. Although he is not active in a church, Maria's daily witness had touched his heart. He was charmed by Lillian's beautiful china cups, the piping hot coffee, and the lively conversation. He listened when John read from God's Word and they prayed together.

Dr. Sue Lee, formerly one of John's citizenship students, also came and brought two of her young daughters for their regular Christmas visit with the Isaacs.

Dr. Lee had studied Bible in the international Sunday School at First Baptist, Tallahassee, before she started citizenship classes. Martha Wheeler transported her and her children each Sunday. Lillian had given Bibles to the children. John and Lillian visited her often and invited her husband, Henry, to attend the class for internationals also.

One Sunday Henry said, "I am going to join the church today. Will you be there? You and the Sunday School class are a part of the reason I want to join, and Sue is the other part. She has lived a Christian life before me. I can see a difference in her. I have been a Buddhist, but now I want to be a Christian." Sue and Henry joined the church and were baptized together.

After Sue and her daughters left, the art lover returned with his older son. He wanted this son to meet Johnny. The boy seemed impressed with the new Bible Lillian had given him and promised to read it.

Christmas Day was on Sunday. It was cold, unusually cold for Florida. To make matters worse, the Isaacs' big hall heater refused to work. Sweaters

194

and the heat of the kitchen stove made the chilly air bearable. John and Johnny entertained their "Christmas stranger" in the living room while Lillian prepared Christmas dinner. Every year the Isaacs invite someone to eat with them who might not have a Christmas dinner otherwise. By the time dinner is over, the stranger has become a friend. One of the internationals from First Baptist, Tallahassee, had come home with them this Christmas.

Before time to eat, Faye Cupit called. She had moved away from Tallahassee but called each year at Christmas. She told them she was attending church regularly and serving as a pink lady at the hospital. She thanked John and Lillian for their prayers for her and for opening the Bible to her and to Max.

Soon Lillian's family arrived with a beautifully baked turkey. Lillian, with Johnny helping her, hurried to put the finishing touches on the rest of the dinner. John introduced their new international friend, and all gathered at the table. John blessed the food, and the sounds of family chatter and Christmas laughter warmed the room.

But Christmas was not over. Chin Sun Stevenson; her husband, Steve; her college-age son and daughter; and 12-year-old Lucas were to visit the Isaacs on Monday. This Alaskan family was visiting in the Lower Forty-Eight and stopped in to spend the day with the Isaacs.

Johnny and Chin Sun's children left to see the city, while Chin Sun and Steve settled down at the cool house for the day. Chin Sun said, "Mother Isaacs, I have so many unanswered questions. Can we just spend the day reading God's Word and praying? No cooking or bother with anything—go out to eat—talk and read and pray?"

Chin Sun sat close to Lillian as she asked her questions and they searched the Scriptures for answers. The presence of the Lord was real to both couples.

Later they talked about the Korean church in Anchorage, and asked the Isaacs to pray that a pastor be found soon.

"You'd be proud of Chin Sun, Mother Isaacs," Steve volunteered. "She speaks for us at the services until we find the right pastor. And people are being saved every Sunday."

"We are proud of both of you. We have already heard about your good work there," said Lillian.

The Stevensons seemed to draw strength from the time with the Isaacs. They prayed and cried, and laughed and shared together. No such visit is ever long enough, but there was time to wait on the Lord and read His Word to find answers for Chin Sun's questions.

The repairman came late in the afternoon and repaired the heater. Soon the house was at a more normal temperature. But that did not matter so much. John's and Lillian's hearts were still warm with the afterglow of love shared at Christmas.

John and Lillian, now retired, stand in front of their first home in Kentucky.

John and Lillian return to visit Clear Creek Baptist School (1983).

John returns to Kentucky to visit Fonde Baptist Church, one of his early pastorates.

19
Today and Onward

SOMEONE once said, "The importance of the Isaacs' ministry has been in multiplying themselves." Like the ever-widening concentric circles made by a pebble in a quiet lake, the influence of this chosen team has moved far beyond their knowledge and even beyond their imagination. God in his goodness has permitted them to see some of the harvest from seeds they planted and cultivated. Occasionally they can see even another harvest from that first yield.

The Isaacs visited Clear Creek in 1983. A young man walked up and shook their hands.

"My grandmother learned to read when you were here, and it changed her life. When she first started to learn I read the Bible to her every day. Her fingers followed the words in her own Bible. Then one day she could read better than I could. From then on, she read the Bible for herself. She never missed a day reading from the Word."

"And what is your name?" John asked.

"Why, I'm George."

"And who was your grandmother?" Lillian asked seeking another clue.

"Ruth Shepherd."

"Are you *the* George who rode with us to Oneida that day when your grandmother gave her testimony?"

"One and the same."

"Do you remember anything that was said that day?"

"I remember everything that was said!" George began to recount some of the conversation. He knew the exact verses his grandmother had read. He remembered her joy in reading. And he remembered the pride that he, as a 12-year-old boy, had felt in her accomplishment. "The last thing Grandmother did before the Lord took her to be with Him was to read her Bible."

"What are you doing now, George?" Lillian asked after a moment.

"Why, the Lord called me to preach, and I'm here at Clear Creek studying."

"That's wonderful! I know your grandmother would be proud of you!" said Lillian.

"Yes ma'am, she sure would. And I go every week to the jail to teach those guys there who can't read yet."

Nearby in Whitesburg, Kentucky, Ruth Addington Baker and her husband, Ed, live and work in their local church. For many years, Ruth has taught preschoolers about missions. She uses her vast missions reading background to widen the worlds of the children in her group, and continues to read for herself.

The Isaacs visited Fleming, Kentucky. David Lyons preaches in the same hills where the Isaacs labored. David and his wife, Sue, were in the first literacy workshop at Clear Creek, and continue to open the Word of God by teaching persons to read.

In 1983 the Isaacs also saw in action the English-Citizenship School at Grandview Baptist Church in

Anchorage, Alaska. For 21 years that school has provided instruction to more than 2,500 students from 69 countries of the world. (It rivals the record of the school in Fairbanks, now in the capable hands of Nancy and David Baldwin.)

Louise Yarbrough said, "Literacy missions came to Alaska in the hearts of John and Lillian Isaacs. Not only did the Isaacs begin literacy mission in Fairbanks, but they were the inspiration for its beginning in Anchorage."

Both schools continue to grow. Lillian and John have met scores of people over the Lower Forty-Eight who were touched for the Lord in Fairbanks and Anchorage. And again the Lord allows them to see some of the harvest.

Chin Sun Stevenson dreamed of a church for the 3,000 plus Koreans in Anchorage. Today, the church is in operation and they have called a pastor. Chin Sun still depends on the Isaacs' prayers.

Gracie Huff teaches in the Monday night Bible study program for children at Friendship Baptist Mission. A passerby can hear her say, "You have said your verses so well! Tonight I have a special verse for each of you. Learn God's Word! Hide it in your heart. He speaks to you through His Word." She sounds much like her role model, Lillian Isaacs.

John and Flora Klepac and Sam and Betty Gilson are only two of the military couples who continue to work for the Lord. Sam and Grace Faulkenberry and countless summer missionaries like Cathy Belew (now Cathy Belew McGraw) widen the influence of the Isaacs.

In Florida, John and Martha Wheeler, Rev. Lofton, and Rev. Davis extend the long list of fellow workers who count their lives blessed by the Isaacs, and in turn pass on the blessing.

When John began to teach for the seminary extension, he had to decide which book of the Bible to teach. John chose Genesis. Twelve years later in the fall semester, he taught the book of Revelation. Several of his students have studied through the entire Bible with him. Others who started later look forward to completing the cycle as he starts at Genesis again. These students, many of them pastors of churches in northern Florida and southern Georgia, preach the Word each Sunday as John has taught them.

Maria, Custodia, Tadako, and dozens of other internationals spread their new knowledge of the Word in their homelands when they visit.

In the spring of 1984, Lillian was making a trip to Atlanta. Before she left home, she and John prayed that she could be used by God on the trip.

At first no one sat beside her on the plane. Lillian was beginning to think the trip would provide a quiet time for reading.

Then a young man, unshaven and distracted, sat down. Attempts at conversation were nearly futile. Lillian did discover that Medhi was going home to Morocco. He was a student majoring in math at Florida State University. She could see he looked desperately unhappy. She began to pray for him, offered him a newspaper, and prayed again. Medhi refused the paper. He also refused refreshments from the stewardess.

When all approaches were rebuffed, Lillian thought maybe she should leave him alone. But a voice whispered to her, "Try again."

Lillian smiled and said, "You must be a very smart student to major in math. God has given you a wonderful mind. He loves you so much!"

A tiny quizzical smile crossed Medhi's face. He excused himself and moved toward the lavatory. Lillian prayed. Just a few moments later, the young man returned. He faced Lillian squarely, "I just went to the rest room to end my life, but I couldn't do it." He opened his fingers to show a handful of pills. "Something made me come back and talk to you. You said that God loves me. I don't know! Are you sure?"

Lillian prayed as she talked about God's sure love. Medhi seemed to want to believe her. She gave him her phone number and address. "When you come back to Tallahassee, call me. I want you to come to my home and meet my husband and son."

Medhi stared at Lillian. "Why are you doing this for me?"

"Because God loves you, and I love you," Lillian replied.

Although the plane circled Atlanta for 20 minutes after the short flight, there was little time to finish talking. But there was help. Lillian reached into her purse to get the tracts she had brought, and a Scripture portion of John. "These are for you, Medhi. Read this book every day. It is God's Word. He speaks to you when you read it. And even though we go our separate ways in Atlanta, I will pray for you every day."

"You will pray for *me*?"

"Yes, I will. Some friends will meet me at the airport. They are Christians, and they will pray for you too. God loves you, Medhi."

By now Lillian and Medhi were inside the airport. He reached for her hand, shook it, and left to catch his international flight. Almost out of sight, he turned, held up the little book, and shouted, "Every day."

"I have planted" (1 Cor. 3:6a) Lillian thought, "and I will pray for Medhi and his family until he returns."

John and Lillian Isaacs opened a new door in 1958 when they, as Home Mission Board appointees, tied the cause of literacy to the cause of missions. In so doing, they launched another way for

Southern Baptists to make God's Word known to everyone. And to their own lifestyle of proclamation and personal witnessing they added teaching adults—poor readers, nonreaders—to read for themselves the Word of God.

Ellis Easterly, of the *New Orleans Times Picayune* and editor of *The Middlesboro Daily News* when the venture began, says, "It is a wonderful thing to teach a person to read. But when a Christian teaches a person to read, a whole new dimension is added. As the new reader identifies with his teacher, he sees the difference that Jesus makes in a life. He is introduced to the Word of God, and the witness of the Holy Spirit in his heart can produce an incomprehensible result—a new Christian."

John and Lillian talk with George Shepherd, Ruth's grandson, on a visit to Kentucky.

Lillian (left) and Mildred Blankenship (right) lead a literacy workshop (1976).

Nell Tyner Bowen was born into a pastor's family and grew up in the church and its organizations. She graduated from Tift College in Forsyth, Georgia, with majors in music and English. She also studied at the School of Church Music at Southern Baptist Theological Seminary in Louisville, Kentucky. While at seminary Nell met I. W. Bowen III, a doctoral student. Nell and I. W. married, and I. W. took a teaching position at Tift College. Their two children were born and grew up in Forsyth. After 28 years of college teaching, I. W. entered the pastorate. Since 1979 he has been pastor of the First Baptist Church of Barnesville, Georgia. Nell teaches music and Sunday School and works with Acteens.

Nell has served as Georgia WMU president (1970-1975), and as a writer for several WMU periodicals. She is the author of *The Seeking Woman I Am* and *The Woman I Am*. She also wrote *Southern Yankee*, the 1965 Home Mission Graded Series book for Intermediates. For two terms she was a member of the Home Mission Board.

John R. L. Isaacs XV, known as Johnny in this book, illustrated the cover for the biography of his parents.

John was born in Fleming, Kentucky, and at age six moved with his missionary parents to Fairbanks, Alaska. He received his earliest training in art from the famous Alaskan artist, Clara Fejes. His grandfather, John Isaacs XIII, was also a teacher and artist. This family background has had a strong influence on John's artistic inclinations. John believes the arts serve as a vehicle for self-expression, especially the visual arts.

John earned his bachelor's and master's degrees in education from Florida State University and has taught elementary school. He now resides in Tallahassee, Florida, where he has been a teacher of adult basic education at the Federal Correctional Institution since 1979.

Order Form

Eagles Publishing Company
384 Bullsboro Drive # 339
Newnan, GA 30263
Phone: 770-252-4356 Fax: 770-502-0281

Yes! I'd like to order additional copies of

"John and Lillian Isaacs: Making the Word Known"

Order online at www.eaglespubs.com or:
Fax this form to: 770-502-0281 or
mail this form to the above address.

____ **copies at $ 11.95 each** $ _____
Shipping and handling $3.00 for 1 copy $ _____
Shipping and handling $4.00 for 2 copies $ _____
Shipping and handling $5.00 for 3 copies $ _____
Shipping and handling $6.00 for 4 copies $ _____
Shipping and handling $7.00 for 5-7 copies $ _____
Shipping and handling $8.00 for 8-10 copies $ _____
GA residents add 7% sales tax $ _____

Total order $ _____

Make all checks payable to Eagles Publishing Company

Charge to:___VISA   ___Mastercard

Account no. _____

Signature _____

Daytime telephone _____

Order Form

Eagles Publishing Company
384 Bullsboro Drive # 339
Newnan, GA 30263
Phone: 770-252-4356 Fax: 770-502-0281

Yes! I'd like to order additional copies of

"John and Lillian Isaacs: Making the Word Known"

Order online at www.eaglespubs.com or:
Fax this form to: 770-502-0281 or
mail this form to the above address.

_____ copies at $ 11.95 each	$ _____
Shipping and handling $3.00 for 1 copy	$ _____
Shipping and handling $4.00 for 2 copies	$ _____
Shipping and handling $5.00 for 3 copies	$ _____
Shipping and handling $6.00 for 4 copies	$ _____
Shipping and handling $7.00 for 5-7 copies	$ _____
Shipping and handling $8.00 for 8-10 copies	$ _____
GA residents add 7% sales tax	$ _____
Total order	$ _____

Make all checks payable to Eagles Publishing Company

Charge to:___VISA   ___Mastercard

Account no. _____

Signature _____

Daytime telephone _____